OPUS 1

ALSO BY W.D. JACKSON

THEN AND NOW

Selection from *Opus 1*:
    Aesopean (Shoestring Press)

Selections from *Opus 3*:
    Boccaccio in Florence and Other Poems (Shearsman Books)
    A Giotto Triptych (Shoestring Press)
    Afterwords (Shoestring Press)

Opus 3 (Shoestring Press)

THEN AND NOW

OPUS 1

W.D. JACKSON

All rights reserved. No part of this work covered by the copyright herein may be reproduced or used in any means – graphic, electronic, or mechanical, including copying, recording, taping, or information storage and retrieval systems – without written permission of the publisher.

Printed by imprintdigital
Upton Pyne, Exeter
www.digital.imprint.co.uk

Typesetting and cover design by The Book Typesetters
hello@thebooktypesetters.com
07422 598 168
www.thebooktypesetters.com

Published by Shoestring Press
19 Devonshire Avenue, Beeston, Nottingham, NG9 1BS
(0115) 925 1827
www.shoestringpress.co.uk

First published 2023
© Copyright: W.D. Jackson

The moral right of the author has been asserted.

ISBN 978-1-915553-31-7

Cover image: Arturo Di Stefano, *William Brown Street, Liverpool*, 1994
Oil on linen, 167 x 197.8 cm (private collection)
© Arturo Di Stefano, 1994
Reproduced by permission of the artist

CONTENTS

Author's Prologue   4

Opus 1, No.1: Self-Portrait as a White-Collar Worker (1) – From Hand to Mouth

1. Difficulties of a White-Collar Worker   9
2. Heinrich Heine: *Deutschland. Ein Wintermärchen* (ll.1–48, 77–120)   12
3. From Hand to Mouth. *Or:* Snowed Under   15
4. Heinrich Heine: *Das Sklavenschiff*   21
5. The More the Better   28
6. Intimations of Mortality from Recollections of a Recent Holiday   30
7. The Gift of Tongues   31
8. A German Childhood. *Or:* Forms and Forces   33

Aesopean (1)

Opus 1, No.2: Self-Portrait as a White-Collar Worker (2) – Words in the Dark

1. The Progress of Truth   47
2. Heinrich Heine: Forms of Fall   50
    - i *Adam der Erste*
    - ii *Untergang der Sonne*
    - iii *Götterdämmerung*
    - iv *"Es träumte mir…"*
3. Paradise Island   59
4. The Park on Sunday   64
5. In Lieu of a Manifesto: Heine's Grave   70
6. At Home Among Strangers   84
7. Words in the Dark   86

Aesopean (2)

Opus 1, No. 3: Interpretations

1. Hamlet in England   103
2. A Bohemian Painter Looks Himself in the Eye   112
3. A King and Not a King   116
4. Picasso's Children. *Or:* Ways of Seeing / Ways of Saying   119
5. Thirty-Nine Songs *(ca.* 1250 / 2002)   125

6	The Bride's Story	150
7	The Two Sons	161

An East / West Epilogue

1	Aesopean (3)	169
2	Nathan the Wise – A Medley	175
3	Aesopean (4) – After Chuang Tzu	193

Acknowledgements and Notes   201

THEN AND NOW

*History, Stephen said, is a nightmare from which
I am trying to awake.*
       James Joyce, *Ulysses*

*Rose, o pure contradiction, desire
To be no one's sleep under so many
Eyelids*
       Rainer Maria Rilke

The world is led by mind.
       Gautama Buddha

OPUS 1

OPUS 1 – AUTHOR'S PROLOGUE

"Events are our masters" – Pascal

"Thought seeks to become action, the word to become flesh… The world is the signature of the word" – Heine

Reader, no matter where or when
The events which rule our lives occurred,
This book can only live again
If you choose to let each silent word
Resound here now in rhythm and rhyme.
In any place, at any time
We take our choices. Or they are
Taken not by but for us. We
Are the victims – or not – of history:
Of parents and family, *shouldn't* or *should;*
Of Jehovah – Jesus; Evil – Good;
Poverty – wealth; of political war
Or politic peace. From the sublime
To all the sick, ridiculous
Jokes chance happens to play on us:
Our loves, our hates, the social mores
Which tell us how to live our stories –
Tell us, in 1997,
Now God's no longer in his Heaven,
And we only live once – so 'self's the man' –
To get rich quick, or grab what we can –
To kick, bite, trample, arse-lick, run
Faster and faster, since winning's fun –
Though *then* remains forever ahead,
As well as behind. This blind, reductive

Race to the land of milk and honey,
This bright idea of the living dead –
'The more, the better' – more power, more money,
Possessions, pleasure – ignores how *enough*
Is choked and poisoned by *too much*,
As murder is always self-destructive,
Or clenched flesh dies in its own clutch.
But we live here, no matter where
Events have taken / will take place;
And we live now, no matter when
We fell – or did not fall – from grace.
At another time in another place
The family – tribe – caste – village grew
Like a tree whose roots and branches knew
Of light and dark and the changing seasons
But had no need of abstract reasons,
Unlike this glossy machine-age, cursed
And crazed with the need to justify –
Allure with carrot – threaten with stick:
We make ourselves – and others – and, worst,
The very world we live in – sick!
But we all join in – act or react
In fear or anger. How to remain
Human – or even not inhumane –
At such a time in such a place,
Is my only theme that matters. How
To release from the bloodless there of then
The here – the power – the peace of now
Is the entire responsibility,
Burden and opportunity –
Absurd – obscure – frightening – free –
Of each small soul. To let oneself be,
To go one's way, re-dream one's dream,
Creating the values time-tied men
Have destroyed or lost or merely lacked;
Also to choose one's style for each theme,
Whatever 'the age demands' – is to set
The teeth of the age on edge. This set
Of pieces – these first words on the way
In search of peace amid the strife
Which "this strange disease of modern life"
Afflicts our world with – try to get
A mind's-eye view of what's gone wrong.

Reader, it's never *all* in the mind,
But since art's what we make of what we find,
And since we also see what we say,
I've tried to make these fragments fit
Into a pattern – hardly a song.
I wonder what you'll make of it,
As we make or 'read' our world – translate
Its sounds and signals. Life-artists let
Live and let flow, let the outer grow
Into an inner, imagined thing –
Transformed, not falsified. And yet
The world remains beyond us. Although
We may choose how we see, the thing we see
Is an image – no more – of reality.
And though there's more to come – of my life
And of the work, that husband-and-wife
Duet – no human being can know
What horror or beauty events may bring
Over the hill or round the next bend.
Or where and when the way will end.

(1997/2001)

Opus 1, No.1: Self-Portrait as a White-Collar Worker (1) – From Hand to Mouth

> *… Caesar's double-bed is warm*
> *As an unimportant clerk*
> *Writes I DO NOT LIKE MY WORK*
> *On a pink official form…*
>   W.H. Auden, *The Fall of Rome*

1   DIFFICULTIES OF A WHITE-COLLAR WORKER

"You appear, like me, to lead a very exhausting life, with the leisure that you want always a mirage ahead of you, your holidays always disturbed by foreseen (or unforeseen) calamities... What I do – I am dealing alone with all the debts and claims of the bank under the various Peace Treaties – sometimes takes a good deal of thought and strength... The chief drawback to my present mode of life is the lack of continuous time, not getting more than a few hours together for myself, which breaks the concentration required for getting out a poem of any length."
– T.S. Eliot to John Quinn, 9 May 1921

WRITE what shall I write?
Who have sold my mind – into legal employment
By an electronic communications multinational
Having its headquarters in the Federal Republic of Germany
And offices, factories and subsidiaries in:

> 28 countries of Africa
> 24 countries of North and South America
> 32 countries of Asia and Australasia

and

> 26 countries – including 31 locations in Britain
>   alone – of Western and Eastern Europe.

Write write what shall I write? Whose father,
Arthur Edward Cyril Parker, was appointed telephone operator
In the London offices of Faber & Gwyer, publishers,
At approximately the time that Mr Eliot joined the company
At a salary (my father
Not Mr Eliot) of one pound ten a week
Rising, by annual increments of five shillings –
Mr Eliot was a stickler when it came to figures –
To two pounds ten a week; with a bonus of thirty shillings at Christmas
And one week's leave a year.

Here is a row of writing desks, orderly files, all looking remarkably multinational,
Remarkably like each other, lit up by a neon flare
Of energy inexhaustibly supplied
By I cannot tell how many miracles of technology.
What shall I write? As one of so many
Crowding the way. As the long-lost son
Of one of the low,
Of one of the least of a statesman's difficulties,
Who fathered six children and later returned to Liverpool

– Or Bradford – or even stayed where he was in London –
And raised his children in another statesman's difficulty
Long overdue for clearance down by the river.

Father father (not among these necks
All correctly attired)
I a tired head
Among these heads
Who said right out loud, *crumpets*
In church on Easter Sunday,
Who threw away that sausage.
Father

As a difficult child
I was naturally subjected
To fourteen years of schooling, and learned
That one does things in order. For example,
One learns things in order
To pass exams and/or become employed
Which is what one lives in order
To do. So I laboriously studied
German – or Law – or Physics – or Engineering –
Or even Business Administration –
At the state's expense. After which I was appointed
At exactly what salary I have never been able to calculate
To the ranks of our company's myriad-minded middle-management
And my thoughts were no longer free
Of charge. Languages
Have always been highly saleable on the job-market
Like muscle on a slave. How should I write
Understanding so little
I a tired head among these heads
Understanding so little –
Late evenings
And one month's leave a year
To relieve my mind
Of the boredom and fear
Which oppress and upset it.
"Fool," said my boss to me: "Poetry's a mug's
Game. Forget it."

Afterthought

"Or, if you really must, why not choose something great
And preferably entertaining –
Look in your bank-book
And write! – to translate?"

2 HEINRICH HEINE: *DEUTSCHLAND. EIN WINTERMÄRCHEN* (ll. 1–48, 77–120)

November it was. And the cloudy skies
Grew daily more down-hearted;
The wind tore at the leaves on the trees;
And off for home I started.

And as I came to German soil
My heart seemed to be drumming
Harder and faster. In fact I think
The tears had started coming.

And when I heard my native tongue
I felt so moved for a minute
I thought my blissfully bleeding heart
Would spill all the blood that was in it.

A girl was singing to a harp.
She sang with warm emotion
And tuneless voice, but I felt played
Upon by her devotion.

She sang of love and the pain of love,
Self-sacrifice, re-union
Above the clouds in that better world
Of wholly happy communion.

She sang of this earthly vale of tears,
Of the joys we cannot capture,
Of the life to come where the soul shall feast
In eternal radiant rapture.

She sang the old Forbearance Song,
The Lullaby of Later,
Which keeps the whining lumpen poor
From turning agitator.

I know the method, I know the text,
And I know the likes of the author;
I know that they secretly tipple wine
While openly preaching water.

A new song, a better song,
Companions, I shall write you!
And here and now on earth we'll build
A heaven to requite you.

We want our happiness here and now
On earth: we don't want hunger.
Let lazy bellies squander the thrift
Of hard-working hands no longer!

For human kind down here below
The bread we produce is ample –
And roses and myrtles, beauty and lust,
And garden peas, for example.

Yes, garden peas for everyone!
Come pile up the pods on the barrows.
And leave the promised Bread of Heaven
To the angels and the sparrows.

***

And while the little singer played
And panted after election,
The Prussian Customs Police undid
My bags for an inspection:

They poked their nose into trousers and shirts
And hankies, and fumbled for hidden
Laces and knick-knacks. And for books
Whose Knowledge was Forbidden.

O blockheads! poking in my bags
With dumb official diligence:
To confiscate the contraband
Of the mind requires *intelligence!*

There I have needlework finer than
Any of Brussels or Mechlin,
And once I've got my needles out
You won't hear yourselves for heckling.

And I carry knick-knacks in my head,
Jewels to crown and enthrone one,
The holy gems of a *future* God –
A great, as yet Unknown One…

And in my head there are many books:
In fact, more plainly stated,
My head's a singing nest of the sort
You'd like to see confiscated.

Believe me, in Satan's reading-room,
Les paroles ne sont plus dangereuses:
They're twice as dicey as Hoffmann von F.'s
Unpolitical verse!

– A fellow-traveller starts to praise
But somehow in me arouses
Even more distrust of the Prussian State's
Long chain of customs-houses.

"This customs-union," he explains,
"Will characterize our nation –
Will help our divided Fatherland
To full Unification.

"It regulates each outward
Or material undertaking;
Whereas our spiritual unity
Is of the Censor's making.

"He regulates each inward
Error, correcting sinners.
A United Germany we need –
Without us *and* within us."

3   FROM HAND TO MOUTH. OR: SNOWED UNDER
(partly adapted from poems by Ernst Jandl)

"ob die abgebrochene hälfte
immer mit der bestrichenen seite
zu boden fallen müsse

stets mit unlust
betätige er
den kleinen handbesen

derlei trivialitäten
stießen
an den kern seiner existenz!"

— Jandl, *Aus der Fremde*

i

As dawn-clouds the sky,
Cold splattered orts

Of egg and ketchup
Streak his blue plate.

ii

Give —

Since quite so much bread
Seems destined to fall
With the jam-side down

      — him this day his sanity!

iii

With her eyes half-closed
In contentment, the cat –

On patrol in their kitchen –
Ignores his ape-like mien.

iv

He slithers on icy pavements
Past fruitless gardens.

Pegged out washing creaks
On the biting wind.

v

Jammed between steamed-up cars –
With and without passengers –

He makes, for minutes on end,
No progress / no regress.

vi

Old women block his path.
One slips and drops her shopping.

Blood squirts on the dirty snow
From the flesh of an orange.

vii

The butterflies being sick
On his windy corners

Can neither stop nor
Go on. He goes on.

viii

There's a lot he could say
About the work in their office:

They educate managers:
He could dish up a course.

ix

Stapled to uniformity
8 hrs per day,

His mind becomes a warehouse
For files, punches, clips.

x

Discreetly policed
By rules and regimentations,

His thoughts, like frightened citizens,
Conform or leave the country.

xi

By pylons, cables, wires
And switching systems

The secrets of the earth
Shall be netted like fish!

xii

Bangers and mash
With trifle for pudding

Reassure him at lunch
Of the delusions of childhood.

xiii

He eyes the ductile breasts
And tumid ankles

Of the complaisant bar-maid:
How platinum blonde her hair.

xiv

He keeps on meeting
People he doesn't know,

Though they mostly remain
Indigestible.

xv

In the tasteless poppet-chain
Of heads up arse-holes

It's where you spread the butter
That takes the cake.

xvi

2 jars of speeding wallop
Are chased by cops of cuffee

Down the one-way street past his heart
Into the dead-end street of his heartburn.

xvii

The telephone demands
An incisive answer –

Incide and answer!
Outside a dancer.

xviii

His day gets longer
And longer. Or let's say

Shorter and shorter:
It doesn't stretch.

xix

Some people never flip
Their lids. They think that light

And reft have never been
Muxed ip.

Coda

He'd like to be Bad (or Good)
But worries about his liver.

Outside in the snowy wood
Each tree's a careless survivor.

He envies the wren in the wood
And the eel in the depths of the river.

4   HEINRICH HEINE: *DAS SKLAVENSCHIFF*

i

The supercargo Mynheer van Koek
Sits in his cabin reviewing
The wholesale value of his load
And totting up the profit ensuing.

"The rubber's good, the pepper's good:
I've three hundred barrels and sackfuls.
There's stacks of ivory and bags of gold –
But what'll sell best 's the poor black fools!

"Their flesh is firm, their sinews hard
As iron of the finest quality:
Six hundred dirt-cheap niggers of
Guaranteed pure Senegality!

"I swopped them for schnapps and baubles of steel
And beads for their chieftains to toff it in;
If half of them stay alive, I take
Eight hundred per cent profit in.

"If just three hundred stay alive
Till Rio de Janeiro,
I'm promised a hundred ducats a head
From the firm of Gonzales Perreiro."

Mynheer van Koek is torn from his thoughts
Abruptly: van der Smissen,
The good ship's doctor, steps inside
Advising him to listen.

"Well now, sea-surgeon," demands van Koek
Of this leanest of human figures,
Whose nose is full of blood-red warts:
"How are my darling niggers?"

The doctor thanks him for asking and says,
"Mynheer, we can overlook it
No longer: far too many of them
Are starting to kick the bucket.

"Two's been our average loss, but today
Seven joined the powers infernal –
Four men, three women. I've made a note
Of the death-rate in our journal.

"I inspected the corpses with great care:
These rascals have no notion
Of right or wrong – they'll pretend they're dead
Just to get thrown in the ocean.

"I removed the irons from those that were cold;
I change my habits rarely –
And dumped them as usual in the sea
This morning bright and early.

"At once there came shooting out of the waves
The sharks, a whole convention
Of connoisseurs of nigger-flesh;
I think of it as their pension.

"For ever since we left the coast,
Where the ship leads they follow;
The beasts smell out the corpses – and
Sniff – snap – gobble – swallow.

"It's fun to watch the way they snap
At the bodies, one or two angling
In at the head or leg. The rest
Gulp down the bits left dangling.

"And when breakfast's all gone they cheerfully
Tumble around our planking; you
Would swear they were looking you straight in the eye –
Just as if they were thanking you!"

Van Koek breaks in on this fine speech
With a sigh: "How can I lessen
This evil? How can I prevent
Mortality's progression?"

The doctor answers, "A lot of the blacks
Have died of their own doing:
Their bad breath smells so foul that the air
Of the hold's not fit to spew in.

"And many have died depressed, been bored
To death by idle slacking.
A breath of air, music and dance –
And we'll soon send this sickness packing."

"What a splendid idea!" exclaims van Koek.
"My first-class nautical leecher
Is wiser than Aristotle, who
Was Alexander's teacher!

"In Delft the President of our
Society of Tulip-growers,
Though clever, isn't blessed with half
Of your commonsensical powers.

"Music! Music! All blacks on deck!
Everyone hopping and skipping!
And if any black should fail to enjoy
Himself he gets a whipping."

ii

High in the firmament of heaven
A thousand stars are thronging:
Their large wise eyes look brightly down
Like a woman's filled with longing.

They gaze upon the sea which far
And wide lies covered over
With phosphorescent purple mist;
The wavelets lap like a lover.

Not a sail on the slave-ship flaps: it lies
As if it had lost its rigging;
But on deck the lanterns flare to the blare
Of a dance-band's jig-a-jig-jigging!

The captain scrapes a violin;
The boys fetch a tub and thump it;
The cook pipes up on his battered flute;
The doctor blows a trumpet.

A hundred negroes, men and women,
Are shouting for joy and stomping
Like mad in a circle. Clanking chains
Accompany their jumping.

They stamp the deck with furious glee,
And several black beauties, moaning
Lustily, clasp their naked men;
Others are crying and groaning.

The gaoler is *Maître des Plaisirs;*
He whips all less than hearty
Dancers, driving them on to get
More pleasure from the party.

With a rum-tum-tum and fiddle-de-dee!
Up from the depths come nosing
Sea-monsters, woken by the din –
Some drunk with sleep, some dozing.

The dull-brained sharks come swimming up
Until there are several hundred
Staring nonplussed at the ship, where it looks
As though somebody must have blundered.

Perceiving it's not yet breakfast-time
They open their gullets, chawing
The air with yawns and displaying rows
Of teeth you could use for sawing.

With a rum-tum-tum and fiddle-de-dee –
There's no end to the celebration.
The sharks start biting their own tails
In ravenous frustration.

I don't think music moves them much,
Or other beasts which prey so.
"Let no such brute be trusted." Did
Not Albion's poet say so?

With a fiddle-de-dee and rum-tum-tum –
The celebration is endless.
Beside the foremast Mynheer van Koek
Prays to the Friend of the friendless:

"O Lord, for Jesus Christ's sake, spare
My blacks. Should their heathen prattle
Enrage Thee, Lord, please don't forget
They're only foolish cattle.

Three hundred head are all I need
To make the trip a winner:
Spare them for Jesus' sake, who died
For each and every sinner."

***

Three hundred lived – and more. Mynheer
Van Koek retired to Rio.
He built a large white house by the sea
And lived it up con brio.

He kept six slaves to do his will –
Four men and two fine girls.
The men were fit and muscular,
The girls had curves and curls.

In Senegal the French enjoyed
Being carried by slaves on a litter.
He'd brought one on the ship, for four
Big lackeys and one sitter,

With fancy livery for the men,
And a shade for himself when hot.
The pregnant girls stayed in – cooked – cleaned –
And hatched a wicked plot.

His neighbour was a Catholic priest
From Lisbon – an avid reader
Of Virgil, Ovid, Phaedrus. The last
Was a former slave, then freedman.

The priest forewarned him with a tale
Which Phaedrus wrote in verse.
Van Koek refused to listen. He
Ended up rather worse

Than Phaedrus' cock – who'd also enjoyed
Being borne aloft on a litter,
By four black cats. A fox from the wood
Advised him he might do better

To strut by himself: Observe their eyes,
Their claws and teeth. I'd say
They carry you round the dunghill not
As master but as prey.

The cock replied, Well, Mr Fox,
I'm not that stupid. You
Also have claws and teeth... Without
As much as a doodle-doo,

One evening behind that hill of dung
The cock was torn to bits
And eaten by the cats... Van Koek's
Remains were found by some Brits

From Liverpool, who quickly buried
That horribly sorry sight.
They'd fought the Dutch at sea – but no one
Murmured it served him right...

The African slaves all disappeared:
The jungle was deep and tropical.
In the Age of Revolution such
Events were all too topical:

How are the mighty fallen. *The priest,*
With these ancient words as his text,
Remarked that Phaedrus declined to say
Who sat on the litter next.

5   THE MORE THE BETTER

The following poem was written some time in the 1970s. It first appeared in a small magazine in the early '80s, after which I lost track of it for some years. In that time I as good as forgot what had prompted it. Since its reappearance I have discovered, somewhat to my embarrassment, that its ostensible subject was in fact the Bradford businessman Percy Shaw (1890–1976) – who invented not "the bead which lights up traffic signs", which existed already, but the 'cat's eye', which made use of similar reflectors, for lighting the way along roads in the dark, thereby preventing, by common consent, innumerable nocturnal accidents throughout the world. Moreover, as the last of fourteen children still at home, he felt he should look after his elderly parents until they died, and so never married but was happy to remain, in his own words, a "ladies' man" whom the ladies were happy to be with. He owned neither "mansion" nor "grounds", choosing instead to stay in his parents' house (where he had lived from the age of two) until his own death… I include the poem here as evidence of how, if sufficiently distracted – whether by work or other factors – the mind can be induced to mistake for an 'objective correlative' of meaningful thoughts and feelings what may be no more, as Eliot said – to compare my whimper with his bang – than "a piece rhythmical grumbling", i.e. a misrepresentation of reality:

      Twelve televisions, bought not rented,
      Deliver the News in two straight lines
      To the lounge of the magnate who invented
      The bead which lights up traffic signs.

      His mates in flat caps find it funny,
      Though some of them think it's going too far;
      And yet it shows again how it's money
      Makes living standards what they are.

      And Hockneys, Caulfields, Joneses, etc.
      Are stashed away under lock and key.
      He considers, supping champagne, how to better a
      Life of increasing ennui.

      Now that they could afford to have children,
      His wife's all grumble and no grunt.
      The way she goes on at him 's bewilderin' –
      What more does she bloody well want?

She's got her car, she's got her kitchen.
Kids just grow up and go away:
So what's the point? Her permanent bitching
Has turned him prematurely grey –

Like a cat, she says, in the dark. She goes
To a Writers' Workshop. Mills & Boon
Have accepted a 'formula' romance. Who knows,
She might be rich in her own right soon.

She can't stand swots or stuck-up pseudos
Who reckon art's for the sake of art
Or refers to itself (or something). Kudos
And royalties fire her simple heart.

Poetry's a mug's game. Some believers
In taking, though, grow tired of things
And take their lives – as though crying "Relieve us
Of trying to fly with unclean wings!"

So hundreds of Jesus-freak fanatics
Die for an ex-champ boxer who
Owned 18 Rolls Royce automatics
Till Jesus told him what to do.

And after her 22nd novel –
And 13 million sold – the wife
Withdrew to an un-Romantic hovel
In their mansion's grounds. Her burnt-out life

Was prolonged by drugs and private nurses.
Her husband had her certified;
Re-married and, despite her curses,
Was blessed with sons before he died.

6 INTIMATIONS OF MORTALITY FROM RECOLLECTIONS OF A RECENT HOLIDAY

While its well-off owners still think of us as friends,
    We've wangled a winter holiday together
In a high old farmhouse near where Austria ends
    In Czech barbed wire and ragged Asian weather,

And it reminds me of reading Wordsworth as a youth
    "In the great City pent". For now we're free
And the earth is all before us. Here where truth
    May "wake to perish never", here in the lee

Of massive stones stacked low against the cold,
    Where Bohemian winds can blue your baby's face –
Where it's "three seasons winter and one season cold" –
    Which suffer the placid soul to take its place

    Amid spectacular Scandinavian birds
    Awaiting the Northern summer. The herds
Of milch cows quietly, warmly shelter
From the wind whose ice-needles pelter

    The woman climbing the snowy slope.
The blue-faced child in her rucksack regards
A landscape gunned by border guards.
    Faith, love, and hope

    Travel incognito at this border.
The woman brings schnapps, smoked ham and bread
    To our strong stone house – in order

To defend our souls (half-bled
    Of belief) from the colour of cold.

But the bullfinches' wind is red,
    And the eagles' gold.

(1985)

7   THE GIFT OF TONGUES

The baby dreams in her dim bed
Like a warm fruit on a summer night,
As plump and full as if she'd fed
On prelapsarian liquid light;
She rocks on a dumb umbilical tree –
Or so I think of her as we

Relax of a Sunday afternoon,
Listening to music while howling snow
Is hurled outside our window. Soon
The spring will come. But now we go
Lying enarmed, enlegged together
Beyond the wordless rage of the weather –

And beyond the raging words of a world
Where minds are bought and sold to their harm,
Where men and bits of paper are hurled
In a windless, eyeless, endless storm,
Which cannot give, which thinks it can take,
Which can only undo, uproot, unmake

The fragile fruit of infancy,
Till the cold woman and loud-mouthed man
Can only grow in innocency
By luck or some well- or ill-laid plan...
My blood feels crumpled, cold, but your hand
Coaxes it quietly to a stand...

I have been suffering all this week
From a tongue gone brittle earning its bread
By chopping words. Your curious lick
Raises me from the clattering dead,
But your back's still tense. Our silent sex
Fits my concave to your convex

Which I gently stroke and warm with my palms
Till, moving down beneath the covers
I feel you slowly soften. My arms
Encircle flesh which only lovers –
Giving and taking with opening holes –
Soothe with their tongues and tongue with their souls.

8   A GERMAN CHILDHOOD. *OR:* FORMS AND FORCES

"History, Stephen said, is a nightmare from which I am trying
*to awake" – U*lysses

Her charming manner on the telephone
And orderly rows of files at the office
At first seem worlds away from where she learned
That a woman's better on her own,
That whatever praise she's earned
(Though no longer beaten, or burned)
She necessarily suffers.

Our German secretary. Her Nazi father,
She informed my embarrassed wife and me
One evening after wurst and kraut,
Had relished public beatings. Rather
Than watch the prisoners shuffle out
To the crowd's indifferent shout,
She'd pour the beer, or make the tea…

But being his eldest daughter meant she was forced,
Whenever the Russian war demanded men,
To present glum officers with her bouquet
And salute them goose-stepping off. The worst
Was when her father ran away –
Which taught her, she thinks, the meaning of 'betray' –
And her mother refused to mention him again.

And now she has a flat all of her own.
Divorced after twenty years of domestic strife,
Her husband cuts her dead. Three grown-up boys
Are conscientious visitors. Alone,
She makes the most of "little joys".
She seems to think that hope somehow destroys –
But did her duty as a mother, less as wife,

As her mother did before her. When the enemy
Threatened her birth-place with annihilation,
They stayed until the approaching dead
Din of Russian artillery

Forced them to flee. They fled
From danger behind towards danger ahead
In a crawling train without a destination.

Their carriage was an open cattle truck.
So the five children and their stubborn mother
Set off into the cold. At night the rain
Recalls their unrelenting lack of luck:
Afraid, humiliated, trapped again
On that freezing, overcrowded, half-starved train,
She dreams of how they tried to warm each other.

Or wakes pursued by nightmares of disgust
At turnips grubbed with fingers out of mud
Boiled in the baby's potty. And was
It the soldiers' guns or their lust
Which made her scream? So unquietly has
That rape been buried by what is
That what she will still cries for what she would

Do if she could – or would have done – till she
Declares us "mad" to want a second child:
Her English husband claimed his marital 'rights' –
But, surely, with the pill a woman's free…
She hints at the hopeless bondage of those nights,
Of three small children, at the bitter fights
And feeling (for the children's sake) defiled.

She seems to think that artists too are free –
And, oddly, homosexuals. Those who bend
Events to their non-conformist will,
Or do so as far as she can see,
Give her some inner thrill.
She talks from inside herself until
I wonder has she ever had a friend,

If in the office human distances
Don't suit her better – getting machines to do
Without much trouble most of what she wants,
Typing dictations, making xeroxes –

Far from her children's cries and husband's grunts;
Where discipline is tough...
                              But who confronts
Such choices, made without much meaning to?

And how much is chosen *for* us? How can one life
Awake from history's forms and hidden forces?
Each thinks he's different. Aren't we the same?
This woman, I, her husband, my wife:
Who do we emulate, fear, or blame?
And if not, why not? What's in a name?
– Who runs our lives? or sets their future courses?

And what right have I – who hardly know
What I want from what I *don't* want any longer,
Who sell my mind in the same bright place,
Unwilling either to stay or go –
To analyse *her* tied-up case,
(Ignoring the beauty of her face):
Am I more hopeful? freer? stronger?

Aesopean (1)

AESOPEAN (1)

"Aesop the storyteller, our great benefactor, happened to be a slave…"
— *Life of Aesop,* Anon. (1st century, AD)

i

A herdsman showed his quarrelling sons
How hard it is to make
A bundle bend — whereas, in ones
Or twos, sticks easily break.

His neighbour, a merchant, ignored the sticks
But with bundles could always turn
A profit. Or play dirty tricks —
For example, bundles burn.

ii

A poor wild ass inquired of his friend,
A donkey, *how* he'd grown so plump.
The donkey grinned. But his backbone was bent
From the stones he had to hump.

The ass, sneering, chewed a dry thistle.
That night a starving pack
Of hyaenas chewed *him,* skin and gristle.
The donkey rested his back.

iii

Winter. A hungry cicada begged
A colony of ants for food…
— *All summer we gathered grain, thin-legged
Though we are. You sang. What good*

Was that? We worked, you played. It's wrong
To think that God will provide…
But St Francis praised the cicada's song –
And when he died it died.

iv

Before the cat was belled, the mice
Were all for one, one all.
Their elders' sound but unheeded advice
Was *Hide – and* let *her prowl…*

After, they gave up helping each other
And squabbled: which male got more
Females / space / food? And which big brother
Should lead them into war?

v

Enemy soldiers approached a farm –
"Let's leg it," the farmer said
To his donkey, who pondered: *What's the harm?*
I'll work for them *instead.*

I've got two panniers and four good hooves,
I'm sound in mind and limb.
But the enemy army was short of food,
And so they butchered him.

vi

The fox was gone: the grapes still hung
Too high for him to reach.
The Bremen Musicians chanced along:
The cock plucked bunches each.

He liked green grapes. The donkey tried
A few, then munched some hay.
The cat and dog, though, ate them and died.
The fox came back next day.

vii

A vain old vixen had never seen
A lion, until one day
She saw one big enough to dine
On her – and slunk away.

No roar pursued her. They met again –
The lion yawned. When, later,
She dared to hobnob, he shook his mane,
Pounced on her back, and ate her.

viii

(after Goethe)

One winter a mob of frogs – imprisoned
Deep in a frozen pool –
Promised, *If spring returns to free us*
We'll set ourselves to school

Among the leaves and learn to sing
Like nightingales! Spring came.
They paired in the mud – croaked – spawned off-spring,
Sated with more of the same.

ix

One night a fisherman's net was full
Of a large and various catch.
Smart small-fry slipped away. Big dull
Flounders went down the hatch.

A monstrous shark, though, scenting blood,
Snapped up the shoal, capsized
The vessel. Fish and men, as food
For sharks, are any-sized.

x

    (after Grimms' März*chen, No.75)*

A cat encountered a sleek fox
Behind the old Manor Farm
Where recently six at least of the cock's
Dumb wives had come to harm.

You know a lot of tricks, my friend,
She grinned as she shinned up a tree –
I one. But the farmer's hounds, in the end,
Will tear you to bits, not me.

xi

    (after Goethe)

An old and toothless lion invited
The fox and stork to dinner.

A long-necked vase with fish provided
The best of meals for the thinner.

Chicken (not grapes) on a golden platter
Flattered the somewhat fatter.

Each mocked the other's ill-bred manners.
But the lion was no one's fool.

The old being nothing if not planners,
His plan was – *Divide and rule.*

xii

(after Heine)

There are two common sorts of rat:
One hungry and one fat.
The fat rats stay content at home;
The thin and hungry roam.

From continent to continent,
Nothing on earth can, now, prevent
Their progress – nothing sate
Their need to find more things to eat.

*

Their litters swell great nameless groups:
Females are common property.
Their stubborn, rat-radical, foul-mouthed troops
Know nothing of Christianity.

They file on grimly, straight ahead –
Cross mountains, deserts, seas.
If any fall, they're left for dead.
The living carry disease.

*

The fat rats only think of guzzling,
Though some fall prey to sozzling.
While sozzling and guzzling, they do not think
Of the legions of skinny rats on the brink

Of doing the *sort* of damage that
The biggest, wildest, hungriest cat
Could not conceive of. By changing the rules,
They make the wise look fools.

Opus 1, No.2: Self-Portrait as a White-Collar Worker (2) – Words in the Dark

The words of a dead man
Are modified in the guts of the living
    W.H.Auden, *In Memory of W.B. Yeats*

1 THE PROGRESS OF TRUTH

(Written After Watching a TV Production of Berthold Brecht's *Leben des Galilei*)

"Doubt thou the stars are fire,
Doubt that the sun doth move,
Doubt truth to be a liar,
But never doubt I love.

O dear Ophelia, I am ill at these numbers. I have not art to reckon my groans. But that I love thee best, O most best, believe it. Adieu.
    Thine evermore, most dear lady, whilst this machine is to him,
                                                Hamlet." (1601)

After the heretical Galileo
Had ceased to believe his eyes

Other than with the unnatural aid
Of devilish tricky lenses,

Proposing Earth's inglorious progress
Around an unmoving sun –

A star like any other star
(No longer silver, gold) –

And abstract mechanical experimentation
Like a pirate's cannonball

Had probed the still, unprofitable spirit
Of scholastic introversion,

While Paul in his barren grave was busy
Denouncing error and heresy

And blessing the Inquisition which
Was tweaking the unorthodox –

Unracked by doubt, unworried lest dogma
Had naturally nurtured Science

By paving a one-way highway to
The death of myth, the secession

Of outer worlds from inner ones –
It grew to irk more concrete minds,

Or minds less eager to ask how
Than why of mathematics,

Like Hamlet's, or John Donne's, who wrote
"The new Philosophy calls all in doubt;

"The Sun is lost, and th'earth, and no mans Wit
Can well direct him where to looke for it",

That countless things we cannot see
Are true; and countless things

Which the mind has always thought it can see
Are untrue: if what happens

Can be proved not to have happened, if
What doesn't happen can

Be proved to happen; if what is
Is not, and what is not

Is, why, o Galileo, and how –
Having tried our best to believe

That only what's capable of proof
May be believed (the rest

Is hypothetical) – are *we* "To be
Or not"? What *happened?* O,

Now that our world has been relieved
Not merely of myth and magic

But, Mr Galileo, also
Of nicely explained religion,

Please use that enormous brain and tell us
Exactly how to fasten

A bundle of loose hypotheses
About us in such a way

As to bandage the bleeding all-in-each /
And bind the dispersing soul /

Into some *form* of comm/unity —

2　HEINRICH HEINE: FORMS OF FALL

i　*Adam der Erste*

"You sent your policeman down from Heaven
With his sword of flame to bust us,
And harassed us out of Paradise
Without pity, without justice!

"We're outlawed from our native land,
But we shan't regret our marriage.
You can't change the fact that I've enjoyed
The fruit of the Tree of Knowledge.

"And you can't change the fact that now I know
How small you are, a zero,
Though with death and thunder you bang about
Like some universal Nero.

"O God! how pitiful is this
Consilium abeundi!
You're what I call a *Magnificus*
Of the world, a *Lumen Mundi!*

"I for one shan't miss at all
The open fields of Eden:
It wasn't a proper Paradise –
It had trees which were Forbidden.

"I demand my rights, my Liberty!
If I find the least restriction,
For me your Paradise becomes
Imprisonment, affliction."

ii　*Untergang der Sonne*

The beautiful sun
Has gone down peacefully into the sea;
And at once the surging waters are coloured
With the darkness of night:

Only the glow of evening
Still scatters them with golden shimmerings,
And the roaring power of the tide
Pushes white-topped waves up the beaches
Where they hurriedly jump for joy
Like a flock of woolly lambs
Driven by a singing shepherd-boy
Home of an evening.

"How beautiful the sun is!"
Said my friend after a long silence
As we continued along the beach,
And half-joking but half in earnest
He assured me the sun was really
A beautiful woman who'd married
The sea-god out of convenience.
In the daytime she sauntered happily
Across the heavens, dressed up in scarlet
Or flashing her diamonds –
Universally loved and admired
By all creatures on earth,
And gladdening all creatures on earth
With the warmth and light of her glances,
But every evening peevishly forced
To return against her will
Into the cold wet house and barren arms
Of her hoary husband.

"Believe me," my friend continued,
And he laughed – then sighed – then laughed again,
"They're really happily married down there!
When they're not asleep they're squabbling so fiercely
The sea becomes rough on the surface
And sailors can hear in its roaring
The old man scolding his wife:
'You great gaudy eyesore! You
Cosmic courtesan!
All day you're hot for others
But at night, for me, you're cold and tired!'
Well, after a telling-off like that,
What else should the proud sun do
But burst into tears and complain of her misery
So long and so wretchedly that the sea-god

Leaps suddenly out of bed in desperation
And swims up quickly to the surface
To recover his breath and his bearings.

"And that's how I saw him yesterday evening,
Sticking up out of the sea as far as his chest.
He was wearing a jacket of yellow flannel
And a lily-white nightcap –
And had a shrivelled face."

iii   *Götterdämmerung*

> *"Who are these hooded hordes swarming*
> *Over endless plains, stumbling in cracked earth*
> *Ringed by the flat horizon only?"*
>   *– The Waste Land*

The 1st of May comes in with golden lights,
And with a silken gale and scents to inhale,
And tempts us like a friend with snowy blossoms
And greets us out of the eyes of a thousand violets
And rolls a fresh green flowery carpet out,
Woven with sunshine and with morning dewdrops,
And calls together all dear human creatures.
The mindless masses do as they're told at once.
The menfolk get their nankeen trousers on
And their Sunday coats with golden, shiny buttons;
The women dress themselves in virgin white;
Young hopefuls curl or clip their spring moustaches;
Young wenches let their bosoms bubble over;
The local poet puts his pen and paper
And glasses in his pocket; – and off they ramble,
The merry milling mob, out through the gates
And deposit themselves outside on the green grass,
Where all admire the industrious trees' new leafage,
Play with sweet little pastel-coloured flowers,
Listen to sweet little merrily-singing birds
And revel beneath the big blue tent of heaven.

May also came to me. She knocked three times
On the door and shouted, "It's me, the May,

You grey-faced dreamer! Come out and give me a kiss."
But I kept my door double-bolted, and answered
"You shan't tempt *me*, you snake in the grass.
I've seen through you and I've seen through
The ways of this world; have seen too much,
And much too deep – till all the joy's gone out of it
And anger and sickness wrestle in my heart.
I see straight through the stony, callous shells
Of human house and heart, and see the lies
And self-deceiving torment. Condemned
To read the ugly thoughts behind the virtuous
Faces, I see in this modest girl's shy blush
A ruthless hussy greedy with desire,
On that young virile fellow's eager skull
The gaudy cap and bells of a cheated fool!
And all I can see on earth are travesties
And ailing shadows: and how am I to know
If what we're building 's a mad-house or a hospital?
I see through the foundations of the old
World as if they were crystal, and see the horror
Which May with all her merry foliage
Keeps trying to cover up. I see the dead
Laid out down there in narrow coffins
With their hands folded and their eyelids open,
With shrouds as white as their dead-white faces
And yellow worms that burrow through their lips.
I see the son sit down beside his mistress
For the fun of it upon his father's grave;
Around them nightingales sing bitter songs,
And the gentle meadow-flowers' malignant laughter
Sniggers until the dead man turns in his grave
And our old mother, the earth, shudders with pain."

Old earth! I feel you suffer when I see
The red fire burning deep inside your bosom –
And see a thousand veins begin to bleed;
I ache as your old scars split again, burst open
And flame and smoking blood stream wildly out of them!
I see your ancient rock-ribbed brood of sons –
Their huge forms clambering from the dark abyss
Wielding red torches in their barbarous hands; –
They prop their iron ladders up against heaven
Wildly attacking God's citadel; – and dwarfs,

Black ones, climb after them; – and with a crackle
The silver stars of heaven turn into dust;
The golden curtain of God's tent is torn
By impudent hands; and howling hosts of innocent
Angels get thrown down roughly on their faces.
God's face turns livid: he clutches his throne,
Snatches the crown from his head, rips out his hair –
And the unruly rabble crowd up closer and closer.
The giants catapult their flaming torches
Far and wide into heaven; the dwarfs let fly
With flaming whips across angelic backs
Till the angels struggle and writhe in agony –
Get swung around and slung out by the hair.
And now I can see my own familiar angel,
With his golden curls, his lighted countenance,
With everlasting love about his lips,
And everlasting bliss in his blue eyes –
And a disgusting ugly black hobgoblin
Snatches him up off the ground, my pallid angel,
Ogles and mocks his other-worldly body,
Embraces him with a tender, firm embrace –
And a bellowing scream jars through the universe,
The columns fracture, earth and heaven tumble
And crash together, and the old night reigns.

iv   *"Es träumte mir von einer Sommernacht"*

I dreamt it was a moonlit summer-night,
And glorious works of architects and masons
Lay pale and weathered in the gleaming light,
Left over from the time of the Renaissance.

And here and there among the ruins rose
A lonely Doric capital and column,
Scanning the distant firmament, as though
To scorn its thunder: the effect was solemn.

While all about lay broken on the ground
Pieces of portal, statues out of gables –
Sphinx, centaur, satyr: chimeras which compound
The human with the bestial in old fables.

A lidless stone sarcophagus stood bared
Among the debris, quite unmutilated;
Inside the coffin, also unimpaired,
A gently suffering dead man lay and waited.

And caryatids seemed laboriously
To crane their chiselled necks to keep it mounted.
On one side and the other you could see,
In crowded bas-reliefs, old myths recounted:

The great Olympic gods, reigning in pride,
In slothful lust and ignorance of what sin is:
Adam and Eve, carved next to them, supplied
With chaste Judaic-Christian fig-leaf pinnies.

Paris and Helen, Hector and the Fall
Of Troy were there: the city's walls were flaming.
Moses and Aaron stood beneath the pall,
And Judith, Holofernes, Esther, Haman.

The god of love was likewise to be seen,
Phoebus Apollo, Vulcan, Lady Venus,
Pluto, Proserpina, and the Go-between,
Bacchus the god, Priapus and Silenus.

And next to them was Balaam's famous ass –
Bespeaking what the Holy Bible taught us –
Also the test which Abraham had to pass,
And Lot, besotted with his sinful daughters.

Here too was Salome's dance, performed so well
She claimed the Baptist's head – the gaoler was even
Dishing it up… And Satan, sunk in Hell,
While Peter bore the massive key of Heaven.

And, here, were represented one by one
The outrageous doings of Jove, the god of loinage,
Who seduced Leda as a lanky swan
And Danae as a shower of golden coinage.

Here you could see Diana's savage chase,
Her mastiffs and her nymphs with tucked-up dresses;
Huge Hercules making the spinning-wheel race,
His brawn half-hid in female flimsinesses:

And next to them Mt Sinai, veiled in cloud,
And on the mountain Israel with his oxen;
Young Jesus still in the temple, asking loud
Questions to try and trip the orthodox on.

These vivid oppositions paired and jarred:
The Greeks' unthinking joy / the strict theology
Of Judaism. And the ivy twined its hard
Tendrils round both in arabesque biology.

But as I dreamed that I stood musing on
These statues like a sort of poet/boffin,
It strangely dawned on me: I was the man
Who lay there dead inside that marble coffin.

And, stranger still, a most mysterious flower,
Whose violet, sulphur-yellow leaves molested
And charmed my senses with a savage power,
Bloomed darkly at the head of where I rested.

The 'passion-flower' I think I've heard it called
And Golgotha the place where it first sprouted
When Christ was crucified to save the world –
From ground on which his holy blood had spouted.

The flower bears witness to the blood, they say,
And carries in its cup what look like sketches
Of instruments of torture, tools which may
Be used for making martyrs out of wretches.

Yes, everything that anyone could hope
To see a Son of God be made to sample:
The crown of thorns, the cup, the scourge, the rope,
The cross, the nails, the hammer, for example.

And such a flower was bending over me
Where I lay dead, as silent as a woman
In mourning, kissing inconsolably
My corpse with all the kisses she could summon.

And in the magic of my dream the flower
Of sulphur-yellow passion, in the queerest
Imaginable way started to tower
Into a woman – into, yes, my dearest!

You were the flower, yes you, my darling child!
I recognized you from your tender kisses:
No flower's lips ever felt so soft, or wild –
No flower's tears ever burned like my young miss's!

My eyes were closed. Yet with the deeper sight
Which lovers have I saw your face before me,
Glimmering and blessed. In ghostly lunar light
You fixed your eyes on me – as if to draw me.

We didn't speak, and yet my heart perceived
The half-formed, secret thoughts you left unspoken.
The spoken word is shameless. Less deceived,
The purer flower of silence blooms unbroken.

A wordless dialogue! Strange though it seems,
The hours pass quickly in such silent chatter:
The loving small-talk of mid-summer dreams
Woven out of delightful / dreadful matter.

But never ask which matters we discussed! –
Ask the green grass what glow-worms say by glowing,
Ask rippling waves what secrets they entrust
To rivers. Ask the west wind what it's blowing.

Ask the carbuncle what it sparkles for,
Ask roses and night-violets what they smell of,
But never ask the moonlit Passion-flower
Or her dead friend what wordless looks can tell of.

I've no idea how long I dreamt I lay
Surprised by joy in that cool coffin standing
Among the debris. But it melts away,
The peace that passes human understanding.

Only the stillness of the grave can give
Such ecstasy so purely beyond measure:
Our joys are crude and foolish while we live
Our passions cramped, lusts without peace or pleasure.

Yes, even that state of bliss was driven away,
By noises from outside: stamping like cattle,
Two loud-mouthed crowds rushed into dusty fray.
My flower withdrew from that insane word-battle.

I heard a furious, loud, wrangling to-do:
A great debate arose. Nothing could save us.
I thought I recognized a voice or two
As coming from my basso-relievos!

Could *they* be haunted by such bigotry?
Could marble phantoms really be disputing?
Moses' anathemas so savagely
Compete with Pan's wild shouts and pagan fluting?

The True will always fight the Beautiful:
Two human mobs perpetually at variance!
There'll never be an end to the great, dull,
Word-slinging hubbub: Hellenes v. Barbarians.

They cursed, they swore! But none could finish off
The stale controversies, the same old squabbles;
Till Balaam's donkey's brays, like whooping-cough,
Out-shouted both divine and saintly rabbles.

Its nauseous sobbing hee-haws seemed to come
From my throat too: I felt them start to choke me!
At last, in desperation, struggling to stem
The ugly din, I shouted out – which woke me.

3   PARADISE ISLAND

"Pleasure ... generates submission"
– Herbert Marcuse (1964)

The time goes by so quickly:
Already another week!

He sits on the terrace drinking
His wine, too heady to think

But knowing it must be Sunday
Since in families or one by one

Pale strangers arrive, replacing
Brown strangers who've left without trace.

A group gets out of a taxi –
And before they've even unpacked

Their brand-new bags, the children
Are off to the beach, half-wild

To cool themselves, abandoning
Their clothes on the burning sand.

He envies their innocent freedom,
Though here even he feels free

Enough to decide to follow:
The eternal breakers roll

Him up and down in their comfy
Bosoms. The raging sun

Is tamed by perfumed lotions
And stylish glasses, although

Some skins still burn severely.
But a tan is why they're here

And bulging middle-aged udders
And even grandmothers' dugs

Are all hung out. The youngest
Are crying now among

The sun-shades: the sand keeps scorching
Their feet. And swimmers lurch

Across it – plunge in the water
Abruptly. Wishing he'd brought

A novel and not Marcuse's
Abstrusities, he peruses

With imperfect understanding
Pages sprinkled with sand

On the imperfect understanding
Of *One-Dimensional Man;*

But the heat, he soon concludes,
Distracts one's attention. Who

Cares if he ever reads this
Anyway?! What he needs

Is intelligent entertainment,
To help him recuperate,

Not academic abstraction –
Though turning to do his back

He observes their neighbours' daughter
Being pestered by three or four

Unacademic admirers.
The sun sets the blood on fire,

They say: the beach is blazing
With idyllically easy lays

And couples erotically sunning
Their zones. All harmless fun,

Of course, though so much raging
Sex makes him feel his age

And, leaving the beach to Beauty,
They take a taxi to view

A local monastery: religion
Is more relaxing. This fridge

Of a church though is gloomily cared for
By nuns who make it clear

That his wife's 'uncovered'. A farm-hand
Shows more respect. With the charm

Of some prehistoric Golden
Age, he courteously holds

His hat and beads, inclining
His grizzled head as a sign

That he knows of secret places.
The smile on his honest face

As he plucks her oregano
Tempts them warily on

Through pink and green oleanders
To vineyards and olive-trees, round

White houses down to a lakeside:
When they smile in return, and she takes

His photo, he sticks his palm out
For drachmas. *Ah well, no harm*

In helping. Swiftly pocketing
His pickings, he scuttles back

To the church. The lake is shining,
A deeper blue than the sky,

Though its bushy shores are crowded
With tourists, some of them loud

And drunk. Still, here you see Nature
In an almost pristine state:

Its unpolluted colours
Make even the ads look dull.

Which is also why they come here,
Leaving dull home at home,

Where they slave at the office earning
The money they need to burn,

Telling themselves that succeeding
Means getting the things you need –

For instance, another taxi
To take them whizzing back

Along the rugged coast-line
Unfortunately marred by the ghosts

Of unfinished abandoned buildings,
Like lives gone unfulfilled.

But now it's almost evening,
Almost time to eat

At the always friendly taverna
With its almost ethnic fare

Where nothing is ever a problem –
Not even thankless plebs

Objecting to soft tomatoes
In the salad. Sick at heart,

He's glad they'll soon be flying
Back to the grind. Asked why,

He'd probably answer "No comment" –
Even to himself. They'll zoom

In a tube of air-tight metal
Home through the sky, and get

Nostalgic, calmed by their dose of
Pleasure, their paradise

On earth, complaisantly waiting
For next year's holiday.

4   THE PARK ON SUNDAY

"The poet and the dreamer are distinct...
The one pours out a balm upon the world,
The other vexes it."

– These crossed-out lines of Keats' keep running through
My troubled mind. The chestnuts overhead
Like forests painted on a Grecian urn
Have all the stillness that I need to learn:
"Ah, happy, happy boughs! that cannot shed
Your leaves, nor ever bid the Spring adieu..."

The parks where I grew up are not so quiet:
The sticks and stones flew thick again last night
And milk-bottles filled with petrol, fused with rags,
Bombed shops and local business. Shopping bags
Were stuffed with loot. Through smoke and fire-tongued light
An inner-city back-streets mob ran riot.

My birthplace. But not my daughter's. She plays amid flowers
In peacefulness and sunshine. Their scented beds
Are calmly contemplated by the birds
While I, in search of wordlessness – not words –
Gaze at the park's grass-greens, rose-reds,
For such self-regarding hours

As the law might take for 'loitering' in a city
Where if you're young and haven't got a job
They search you publicly, abuse and treat you
Like 'vagrants'; where you're scared they'd beat you
If you gave them a chance. School-children riot and rob
In a no-hope struggle for revenge or pity –

Let down *and* out by overcrowded schools –
Left brainwashed – bribed and bullied into thinking
That the aim of life is work, that work is done
For money, not love; life's no more fun
Than learning, but you might get stinking
Rich if you ply the bribe-and-bully rules...

"How right the workers are," George Orwell said,
"To put the belly before the soul

In point of time." But even if he
Was right in London in 1943,
Now it's the soul that's starved. The police, the dole
Have goaded the neither ragged nor unfed

To an anxious and involuntary flailing
Whose highest motivation is the need
To be issued with regulation fetters
By those they *prefer* to regard as their betters
And with whom they share the easy creed
Which envies strength and blames the weak for failing!

– I stumble against a bench. My daughter plays
Far from the office or from book-shop shelves
Under the chestnut trees. But our favourite park
Appears less peaceful now – less light than dark,
Dark, dark. We blind ourselves, and maim ourselves,
By thinking too precisely on what pays,

On where we're aimed and how we're going,
Till our time-ridden world needs slowing, slowing.

Our movements lose the name of action,
Our satisfactions satisfaction. –

But comfort's still comfort, success success,
And since to be is to possess
The more we've got or get the less
We resent the usual strain and stress;

And poor is poor – humiliation,
Aggro, envy, bored frustration.

Forever struggling to make ends meet –
With your older kids in gangs on the street
And (learning to expect defeat)
Your youngest losing hope at school –
Who wouldn't feel useless or a fool?

Fool! Though the undefeated fly
Beyond the park through the pathless sky
Or sing all Sunday afternoon
(And birdsong is never out of tune),

The word alone reminds me of
So much I'd prefer to be above
On this way of life I'm halfway through
But daily do or fail to do.

And failure's one way to explain
The boredom, the fear, the stress and strain –
Heart trouble – impotence – and cancers.
But we're too keen on one-word answers,

And even hard-and-fast succeeders,
Wine-bibbers, knowledgeable feeders,
Though steeped in the rites and joyless frolics
Of self-respecting workaholics,

Suffer from nameless discontentments –
Sleeplessness – ulcers – confused resentments…

– The Afghan prances proudly by
Which only last Sunday nipped my thigh.
The rosebeds' soil is hard and browned
But my daughter brings a worm she's found,
Which wriggles – as I suppose it must,
Once dropped there – in the sunny dust.

As a child I dreamed of how I'd like
To cycle away on a flying bike.
As if I could rise from my swivel chair,
Fling files and memos everywhere.
As if one could simply leave an office,
Or there were really better offers

Of lives elsewhere. But since there aren't
Or since at any rate we can't
As long as there's no change – no let-up –
In the growth of this self-consuming set-up
Whose masters are its slaves, we resign
Ourselves to falling in the line
Of duty, looting what we can
Since money is what makes the man –
Fiddling expenses, pinching paper,
In on any dodge or caper
That can be cut to fit the tune

We march or crawl to. Picaroon,
Who works to live, who lives to work?
We ought to admit we're in the dark!

But instead we keep on plugging away
Ambitiously from here and now
To imagined deadlines, praise or pay
In an unreal future, ignoring how

The force and lures we all deploy
To obtain what we've been schooled to desire
With quiet legality destroy
Our souls in the great industrial fire:

Fire-blinded and severely burned
Yet ever assured of better health
We gloat that folly and weakness earned
The blue-collar millionaire his wealth;

But are lost in the back-streets. Recently I –
A stranger at home for years,
Informed by the media *where* and *why*
The mob ran riot – have felt goaded by fears
Of why and where my life is aimed,
Felt puzzled again, blinded, maimed.

– Words, *words* we need! The birds which contemplated
The flower-beds hop and scatter now, disturbed
By a loud-mouthed dog. Have I created –
Ever – a peace less curbed, less easily perturbed?
Even the park deceives in its wordless way:
Tomorrow's another working day. All day.

– A *riot* of words! A monstrous, mechanical donkey
Has deafened and hoofed our wordless working world
So long it's turned lop-sided and runs wonky!
If it's not too late, if we haven't been hurled
So far off course there's no way back until
Our greeds and fears destroy themselves. Meanwhile,

It seems that more than one individual
Is sick and tired of insult, feels like spitting
It back in someone's face – as petrol

Or poem. You might as well make shitting
Your aim in life as working for fear or money.
The policeman in the land of milk and honey

Is a measure of how we force our half-bled souls
To knuckle under; the rioters' angry stealing
Of how we lure them. As for other goals
We've long been robbed of words: trained thought, trained feeling,
Cripple our minds. But man is not a beast,
And these street-running rioters cry to be released

From what they cannot think of as oppression
And therefore half-mistake for unemployment
And racist rozzers. A – Keatsian – verbal obsession
With art's unhurried, sure, unending enjoyment
Of seeing the world through freely contemplating
Its mirrored forms would be worth elucidating –

Though Keats himself might stutter – in a place
Where even I, in anger and disgust,
Once smashed a teacher's window. By the grace
Of Sunday School the old gradgrind never sussed
That it was me – the prefect at the front
Who conned his lessons. An isolated stunt,

Which reminds me of the bomb-site where we'd played
At cops-and-robbers with stolen fire as a base
To jump through: daring it, flushed and afraid
We'd be caught and punished. Now, as on Guy Fawkes' Days,
The fires are bigger. But still of the same sort.
If only we could steal back words, steal thought,

Or liberate thought in a riot of words
For each to defend himself as best he can
Against the strait-laced bureaucratic turds
Which'd bed men down in a travesty of man –
A thoughtless, loveless, bribed, tired, bullied brute
In an overall, a uniform, or suit!

Postscript

"Ten red ones," my daughter says. At the age of two,
As she learns to see more clearly how things are
She learns to name them. The roses are "red", not "blue".
But the imagination rarely gets that far!
Perceiving and performing what's been taught us,
We behave like mobs of world- and word-distorters.

Yet every child sees Paradise before
It's kicked in the head by that mad donkey. Later,
"Beauty is Truth, Truth Beauty" is a saw
Meaningless to most of us. But its creator
Knew it might change the world. And if "might" 's not much,
Suffer the little children, for of such

Is faith, hope, love. Like lilies of the field
The children take no thought for the things of the morrow.
But wounds in the mind are only slowly healed
And, wounded, a thing of beauty's dark with sorrow.
My daughter brings a broken rose she's found.
But the chestnuts' roots grope deep in the dark ground.

(1981/1987–88)

5   IN LIEU OF A MANIFESTO: HEINE'S GRAVE

"I am only too aware that my position is unnatural: everything I do is folly to the sensible – and an abomination to the foolish."
– Heine, *Ideas. The Book of Le Grand*

Angrily crossing the Place
   de la Concorde, with the pram
Coming in handy for stopping
   four – five – six lanes of cars,
Poisoning my lungs with their fumes,
   deafening my ears with their din –
Freedom of movement, I thought,
   added a dimension to life! –

We pause at last for a breather
   beside the obelisk where
The guide-book informs us *Madame*
   la Guillotine did her duty
By Louis XVI, Marie-
   Antoinette, Danton, Robespierre,
"Among others" – and try to consider
   how to retreat from this strange

Disease of mechanized life
   up through the streets of Montmartre
Into the silence that grows
   plant-like and motionless where
The named and nameless have lain
   under the yew-trees, famed
Or forgotten, for hundreds of years:
   among *them*, "Heinrich Heine" –

White now, a lyre and poetical
   bust having turned his gravestone
Into a monument, towering
   over a few cut daffodils
(Easter is early this year)
   stuck in a jar at the foot
Of the pedestal, filled by cold
   fresh rain to the flowing brim.

Coldly, sadly the rain
    drips from leafless limetrees
Onto the jumble of graves:
    Far from home, in Montmartre,
Heine lies, who foresaw
    better than Marx, and more fully
Than any English Romantic,
    our 'modern' world and its art:

Rightly he feared us! Although
    'communists' no longer, we
Guilt-ridden, gloomy iconoclasts
    of sublimity, Beauty and Truth,
Have chopped down his laurels and planted
    potatoes – trampled the pale
And idle lilies, the indolent
    roses, for failing to make

A material contribution
    to the good of society. As for
'Philomela' ("piping
    sadly in a grove"),
Most of our generation
    would hardly know if we'd heard her
Jug-jugging her "plaintive anthem" –
    or care very much if we had.

– Afraid that his books would be turned
    into bags for grocers to fill
With the coffee and snuff of the future,
    still he felt bound to accept
That, if the premise was true
    that all have the right to eat,
The world and his art must suffer
    the consequences. Foreseeing

The worst of these consequences
   (with the demons of logic dancing
About him in triumph) – snatching
   the wreath from his brow, awaiting
The fall of the king, in imminent
   danger of losing his wits –
Heine cried out even so,
   "Let justice be done! Our world

Has been weighed in the balance and found
   wanting! And blessed be the grocer
Who turns my books into bags
   for the coffee, potatoes and snuff
Of the age-old women who now
   go gathering fuel to survive
The comfortless winter: *Fiat
   Justitia, pereat mundus!*"

'Communists' no longer – nor fascists
   or anti-Semites (though who
Can honestly say that he
   has never been either? Not
The best – or the most creative –
   among us) – since neither left
Nor right is the thing to be
   at this critical moment in time –

We, the politically correct
   have all been to college, and learned
To do things in order. Our grandparents
   succeeded in selling the grocers
Quite so much produce (potatoes
   included) – in driving such bargains
For the powers and ductile skills
   of their minds and bodies – *or* Mammon,

The glittering god, intervened
   in his usual mysterious way
To perform a *Wirtschaftswunder*
   on their needy behalf – that now
We who were once the lumpen
   poor have made enough money
To pay for an education,
   in order to have a career

As middle-class lawyers or teachers,
   businessmen, hairdressers, artists –
And consume as much as we please,
   or go on expensive holidays
Abroad. While the grocers themselves
   created such scads by selling
Coffee, potatoes and snuff
   to the formerly poor and the rich –

Soapsuds, alcohol, books –
   TVs, cameras, cars –
Electronic commun-
   -ication gadgets and fads –
Constantly changing fashions
   in clothing, music, bikes –
And other such stuff without which
   life has become unthinkable –

Or Mammon the omnipotent god
   intervened on *their* greedy behalf –
That now they've become the richest
   ladies and lords of Philistia –
(A nation of dauntless empire-
   builders, of well-off shop-keepers) –
Seizing the levers of legal –
   political – monetary power…

               *

"Wo wird einst des Wandermüden
   Letzte Ruhestätte sein?"
Has, since Arnold was here,
   been chiselled on Heine's grave.

And yet for two hundred years
   we poets have loudly and proudly
Proclaimed that our books are not paper
   bags of any description,

While slowly, unsurely, retreating –
   some inwardly, others withdrawing
Physically – from here and now,
   at one with Nature – with lovers –

To lakesides, meadows and hills –
   the realm of the free creative
Imagination, *Sehnsucht*
   for the solitary, simple life

Where the noble Savage ran
   As free as Nature first made man,
'Ere Servitude began;
   to the manna and milk of Paradise

(Where all should cry *Beware*
   his flashing eyes! his hair! –
Those sunny caves of ice!
   Weaving a circle thrice):

Retreating from money's rant,
   withdrawing from lack of interest
To visions of unacknowledged
   yet potent legislation;

Turning from turning backs
   to myopic élitism – arrogant
Allusive / elusive obscurity;
   to political resignation –

Art for art's sake, bardolatry –
   art for *my* sake, self-worship –
The egotistical sublime
   disappearing up its own arsehole,

Confusing madness with genius,
   melodious mouthings with meaning;
To arcane and ancient religions,
   inflating egoless egos;

To all-knowing, smart-remarking
   intellectual self-assertion,
Driving out *angst* with hubris,
   chagrin with the salve of renown:

From high Romanticism
   to low Romanticism,
Disassembling formal constraints,
   dismantling 'poetic' personae;

To fantasies, megalomania –
   solipsistic reflections,
Infantilism, melancholy, booze –
   the odd-bod's bog of self-pity;

To affected indifference – the toughness
   of unimportant outsiders –
Badness, gladness, madness –
   suicide, premature death:

A sorry, dishonest spectacle –
   interrupted, it's true,
By brilliant and sometimes brave
   (if self-important) engagement,

Over against the humdrum,
   with whatever's doing the damage
To however we choose to pass
   our time in "this iron time

Of doubts, disputes, distractions",
   benumbing our souls, as in winter;
Of journalists posing as editors –
   editors posing as critics –

Critics posing as poets,
   grinding aesthetical axes;
Of cultural aristocrats who
   market their gifts discreetly;

Of sciolists, pseuds and ruthless
   sons-of-bitches – half-barmy
Bards of suburban Bohemia –
   drug-users, drop-outs, drunks;

As well as of those who, unable
   to outdo the masses, have joined them –
Performers and entertainers,
   blowing their own tin trumpets –

Play-actors, jokers, smart-alecs,
   rappers, slammers and shammers,
Poppers, hoppers, sloppers
   (and, once, a stripteuse artist,

Applauded, cheered and jeered
   by the loud-mouthed crowd): among them,
Hard-nosed publishers – po-biz
   organizers and judges –

Turning poetry into
   an ethereal / material commodity –
Making it *new* – 'New Gen' –
   'new rock 'n roll' – 'New Formalism' –

New trend-setting in-crowds – seeking
   media attention, turning
Grub-street politics into
   a middle-brow song and dance…

                    *

"Wo wird einst des Wandermüden
Letzte Ruhestätte sein?"

'Wo?'

Sick and tired of life's long journey,
Where at last will I recline?
Under mezzogiorno *palmtrees?*
Under limetrees on the Rhine?

Will I lie in some strange desert,
Buried by an unknown hand?
Or may I, beside the ocean,
R.I.P. in coastal sand?

Anyway! God's sky-blue heaven
Will surround me, here or there,
And at night the stars, like death-lamps,
Will attend me anywhere.

And while I mused, night swiftly ran
Across the cloudy sky;
The wind tore at the trees: it began
To rain. And suddenly

A familiar disembodied voice
Was in my ear. It said,
"Poor Matthew really had no choice –
Even though his dad was dead –

"But to tut-tut my one-off sort
Of reckless wit. Sincerely
Fearing to say what he really thought –
Or even to think it clearly –

"Afraid to watch and wait alone,
Or loose the clanking chain
Of such as bluster, cringe and groan
Across the hectic plain

"Of 'modern life', he ran with those
Who *led* the dreary slog,
Policing the herd, keeping them close
Together, like a dog;

"And, like a guard-dog, did his duty
By the holy cow of Culture,
While the dying god of Truth and Beauty
Was torn by the big-beaked vulture

"On John Bull's wrist. The Philistines,
As in his heart he knew,
Had long since won. And pearls before swine
Were all he ever threw.

"At all the sides in man he aimed
And emptily discussed them
Within a conscience bound and maimed
By his mighty father, Rustum.

"'But was it thou – I think,' he claimed,
'Surely it was! – that bard
Whom Goethe' – leaving names unnamed –
'Found gifted but loveless and hard?

"'Love, without which even the tongues
Of angels sound amiss!'
The age demanded love in its songs –
And bared its arse to kiss.

"Such wet-legs with such infant's needs
The powers-that-be found Great
And Good. Such 'love' as theirs concedes
The game to greed and hate:

"A compromise, an abdication
Of responsibility,
An (ig)noble-minded (im)moral evasion
Of whatever it means to be free!

"'In the huge world which roars hard by
Be others happy if they can!
But in my helpless cradle I
Was breathed on by the rural Pan.'

"Innocence fades. It cannot last,
Nor should it. Live here now,
Not in some happy/unhappy past
Or skewed scenario.

"His life and poetry never came
Together. Copping out,
He got a job and married. Tamed,
He burbled on about

"'The harmony from which man swerved
Made his life's rule once more!
The universal order served!
Earth happier than before!'

"In the huge world which roared hard by
He sought and found respect,
And gave up writing poetry
While there were schools to inspect.

"He thought the schools would help each boy
And girl to strive to attain
'One common wave of thought and joy
Lifting mankind again!'

"Whereas all 'common thought' now finds
The poet's life pure folly;
And common 'joy' has gone quite blind
Grubbing for love or lolly.

"The 'universal order' now
Is grab it while you can,
And all the ancient gods shall bow
To democratic man.

"Nor is there any other way,
Since people must be fed.
Some evils now have had their day.
But others have raised their head.

"In the words of a fellow-exile:
  'Such is the structure of life
That what we regard as Evil
  can develop into a fairly
Ubiquitous presence, if only
  because it tends to appear
In the guise of Good. You never
  see it crossing the threshold

"'Announcing *Hi, I'm Evil!*
  The surest defence against Evil
Is something that cannot be feigned
  or faked or imitated,
Something even a seasoned
  impostor couldn't be happy with:
Something, in other words,
  that can't be shared – like your skin –

"'Not even by a minority:
  ideally, a gang of one. –
Evil's a sucker for solidity:
  it always goes for big numbers…'

"In Germany, you see, I learned
  never to trust the poetical:
In earlier times they might have burned
  me and my books as heretical…

"The poet's business is to tell
The truth as far as he
Can see or say it. The victim's yell
Of agony or glee,

"His loves, his hates, his lifelong struggle
To join the crowd, or beat it –
His angry pride – or Arnoldian haggle
To have his cake and eat it –

"His self-assertive song and dance,
His shifting of the blame
To God or Mum-and-Dad or chance,
Though at first they look the same,

"Appear as passive in the test
Of time, which also tells
The truth. For truth is active. Best
Re-dream your heavens, your hells...

"And yet I soon became too ill
To pursue with zeal or zest
The holy grail of man's free will,
Which might have been my quest...

"What Brodsky meant was *Wield your wit
And fight a peaceful war,*
Which is the very opposite
Of crying 'I (won't) withdraw!'

"I understood that neither attack
Nor retreat could in the end
Release me from the turning back
Of enemy or friend –

"That bawling neither *Us and Them*
Nor *All for One...* is free;
That all such slogans also stem
From chains we cannot see –

"And if our world's a gaol of lies,
Or a huge – and growing – derangement,
Perhaps the greatest freedom lies
In unembittered estrangement...

"But I too got lost in that dark age
Of sick fatigue and doubt.
And all my flights of spite or rage
Could never fly me out.

"And so, for myself, I wish
   they'd left me the tombstone that Arnold –
I remember him well, poor Sohrab,
   I remember his mutton-chop whiskers –
Recoiled from in fear and self-pity:
   ' *"Henri Heine"* – 'tis here!
That black tombstone, the name
   carved there – no more!' No dates,

"No epitaph, and no poem:
   that which is nameless may not
Be named, after all – a source
   of 'sweetness and light' to me,
Though of melancholy to Matthew.
   At the end of my days, with *la Mouche* –
The sweet little fly who sang
   about my decaying body –

"I was perfectly happy. Well,
   enough of that. I suppose
Some verses there'll have to be.
   So may I express a preference?" –

   'Jetzt wohin?'

Where to now? My brainless feet
Turn towards the German border.
Common sense, though, shakes its head –
Sets my muddled thoughts in order:

Yes, the war is over now,
But the war-trials are indicting
Such as you, who once, it seems,
Penned some punishable writing.

Well, it's true, a firing squad
Seems a nasty way to snuff it.
And I lack the tragic mien
Which might tell them where to stuff it.

– O to be in England! But
All those sweaty English faces,
Steam and coal-smoke, sicken me,
Causing cramps in several places.

Sometimes I believe I'll sail
Off to Freedom's mighty stable
In the USA, where hicks
Fraternize at any table.

But it worries me that they
Chew tobacco, play at skittles
With no king of any sort
Or spittoon to catch their spittles.

Russia's splendid empire might
Please me better. And I'd dare it,
But the knout in winter, well,
I don't think that I could bear it.

Sadly I inspect the sky
Where a thousand stars are dozing.
But among so many I
Cannot see my own reposing.

Lost perhaps. Astray in heaven's
Labyrinthine golden mystery.
Just as I have gone astray
In the sludge of human history.

6   AT HOME AMONG STRANGERS

With time to kill between the exhibition
Of David Hockney's Lonely Hearts' Club Band
And the start of the play, preoccupied
By images of heroes – boyfriends – fairy-tales –
Elderly parents – C.P. Cavafy –
I make the unthinking mistake (or have I
Become a stranger where I was born?)
Of deciding to go on foot
From the principal tourist attraction
Of this run-down city – a monolithic dock,
The work of insane but fearless giants,
Now cluttered with boutiques and gift-shops
Selling trivia, postcards, confectionery –
Up through the centre of town
Towards the theatre. But
It's Sunday: the new pedestrian precinct,
Stretching into the distance
Like a surrealist vista,
Is deserted and litter-strewn; shut-up shops
And restaurants which might never have opened
Threaten my progress; a group of blacks
Are setting fire to a litter-basket
Outside a fast-food shop; a group of skin-heads
Abuse them obscenely, as I slink between,
Clutching my precious possessions. A police-car
Approaches slowly, like a cruising shark
Through polluted water; the small fry scatter;
And though I pretend I always stroll
Through the heart of the city on Sunday –
Through this cauterized gap in the city –
The police are suspicious: "To the *theatre?*"
I imagine them bawling
In disbelief. But at last I arrive,
Stifling a groan as I realize
This play is the sort of happening
In which you are invited / expected / compelled
To get up and *do* something. The principal actress,
Who has also developed
And now freely-and-easily improvises
The group-therapeutic text, is from New York.

She is moved to tears and raucous laughter
By her childhood memories. So
Is the audience. She unironically believes
In the sexual energy of go-go dancing
And in "democratic communication". So
Do we. She is bored by outmoded classics
Which always take place on stage, as though the actors –
Or any other artist ("they all think they're God") –
Were somehow different. And yet –
So many, many friends
Have died of AIDS!… She wonders
If we can imagine
What that has done
To her. The audience
Is obviously moved
By this moving woman – obviously relieved
By the thought of not being different
Or on its own. She then instructs us
To join in the dancing. The stage is filled
With a heaving mass of bodies. The actress
Removes her clothes to show her sincerity:
Her full-blown figure's past it – but why worry?
Everyone is happy and more than a few ecstatic.
The lights are bright and colourful;
The surrounding darkness is hardly visible.
She obviously loves us. We obviously love her –
Especially those who felt too shy
To get up and dance – including me,
Who have been thinking she might show us
How to walk unafraid through that precinct –
And when she falls off the stage by accident,
Bruising her buttock, a hundred hands
Are ready to help her.

7   WORDS IN THE DARK

"Herwegh, you iron lark!
Like a jubilant bird on the wing,
In holy sunlight you've vanished!
Is Winter really banished?
Is Germany decked with the blossoms of Spring?"
– Heine, *To Georg Herwegh*

They've all gone home. Across the road
The office lights flick quietly out
As Friday evening lightens the load
On all our minds. The latest bout
With time is over. Time has slowed.

Yet boss and secretary must
Still push through patient traffic-jams
Where car-horns, exhaust fumes and dust
Tire harassed mothers pushing prams
With infants who can only trust

That what gets done to them is right,
Or not too wrong, and not a joke.
Striking a momentary light,
I blow a cloud of heat and smoke
In the rough direction of the night.

Four storeys down the lights of cars
Follow-my-leader through the dusk,
As soldiers come from / go to wars –
Or all good students wore subfusc –
Or punk kids follow their punk stars.

All do what everybody does.
I pay my bills – don't stretch my wings –
We're here because we're here because
We're good at putting up with things.
And life feels like it always *was*

The human race heroically
But blindly doing as it's told:
Which must be what I cannot see
At our window – as when, five-years-old,
Our school-class stood excitedly

With thousands lining the road between
The airport and more important places
In that run-down city to see the Queen
Who, travelling on to see the races,
Blessed us from her limousine…

With laughter, aching legs and tears,
Waving one hand, one shoulder touching,
For what seemed hours we practised cheers
In rows by height, like soldiers, clutching
Blue New Testament souvenirs.

Across that road I might have seen
Up a narrow, evil-smelling jigger
With crumbling walls one place the Queen
Would stop. O cathedral! better, bigger
Than either playground or canteen –

Provided you were good. Or tried
To be as good as worthless sinners –
Worthy of punishment for Pride
And other sins concealed within us –
Could be on that blackened riverside.

More sherbet, liquorice, plastic toys,
I thought, rewarded the good as gold
'Above' than in Santa's grotto! "Joys
Await you there. Here all grows old,
Then dies. Be prudent, girls and boys,

And
    'Lay up treasure in Heaven!
    Life will pass away.
    Lay up treasure in abundant measure
    For the great Accounting Day.

  Lay up treasure in Heaven!
  Though men shall be poor,
  Thou shalt reign with the Son of God
  For evermore.'"

Minds moulded by "the old, old story
  Of unseen things above,
  Of Jesus and His Glory,
  Of Jesus and His Love",
Driven on by welcome punishment,
Our lives seem spent on Purgatory –
  "Tell me the old, old story
  As to a little child,
  For I am weak and weary
  And tempted and beguiled":
That sin-heap from the Fundament
Of Man 's a fertile promontory,

We think, from which like twinkling planes
Those blessed with ultimate success
Take off. Their fame, which never wanes,
Dazzles us. Failing to progress,
We fret – and take still greater pains,

As if choirs of ecstatic businessmen
And millionaires in flashy ties,
Exalted by their acumen,
Sang down to us from some Paradise
Of stars and superstars "Amen!"

And so the Queen – like God, whose power
Was also supervisory –
Seemed very good. After an hour
She passed us by. Her stringency
Would turn the milk and honey sour,

And yet we cheer her when she passes –
Defender of the *status quo*
From heresy. The cruel sun-glasses
Of boss or *generalissimo*,
Beaming upon the obedient masses,

Stared from her bright black carapace.
But there was never such a God.
And a pale, stubborn, empty face
And white-gloved hand, waving the rod
We kiss, were all her signs of grace…

And now? High time I went – helped put
The kids to bed. But I won't refuse,
Firstly, another cigarette
And swig of the boss's top-notch booze;
Until I reek of smoke, booze, sweat.

Four storeys down the lines of cars
Go crawling on – from here to home,
As armies straggle back from wars –
Or all roads lead away from Rome –
Or Wise Men tire of following stars.

– Who *chooses* which lines he'll live along?…
The phones on both sides of the road
Are silent now. What sort of song,
As Friday evening lightens the load
On my mind, would *not* feel tired and wrong?…

'An Georg Herwegh'

Herwegh, you iron lark!
Like a jubilant bird on the wing,
In holy sunlight you've vanished!
Is Winter really banished?
Is Germany decked with the blossoms of Spring?

Herwegh, you iron lark!
So high through the sky you fling
You quite lose sight of earthly curses:
Only in your verses
Lives the Spring of which you sing.

Material-minded through and through,
The takers now have taken over
So thoroughly that any who
Is still a giver, liver, lover,
Had better be a liar too –

As Heine was. An honest man,
He might have said, is one who knows
More or less when he's lying – an
Unhealthy running saw to those
Whose mores are more puritan.

Flattering, complaining, wangling, he
Waged life like a one-man guerrilla war
Against a Romantic century:
Destroyed but undefeated, he bore
A lot of painful poetry –

Whose purest patterns neither win
Nor lose but grow in each of us.
But the worst comes to the worst within.
All do what everybody does.
Are these the wages of our sin?

And why should we feel life always was
Redeemed by putting up with things?
I'm here because I'm here because
I pay my bills. My grubby wings
Were formed and clipped by unwritten laws.

The "age demands" role, meaning, style:
Words slip and slide. From behind the fence
Of past and future we revile
And praise in our own self-defence.
The window reflects my defensive smile…

But beyond our worn-out fantasies
Other forms move – of time, of space.
If our oldest stories mould what is,
If the only facts in such a case
Are feelings, dreams, appearances,

We must re-dream ourselves. Like cars,
We twinkle loudly through the dusk,
As whiz-kids follow board-room stars –
Or I and others wore subfusc –
Or soldiers leave for wars – wars – wars…

Though now across this darkened road
I see a tailor's dummy, white
And blind, lean from a black explod-
ed window. But I hope to write
Until my mind and life have slowed.

Aesopean (2)

AESOPEAN (2)

"... a rat is not an elephant"
— Jean de la Fontaine, *Fables* VIII, 15

i

(after Lessing)

A goose there was whose feathers shone
So white she wondered if
She had in fact been born a swan…
Her neck, it's true, was stiff —
And too short, perhaps? When on her own,
She strove to stretch and curve it.
And swanned about the lake alone.
Her flock-mates honked to observe it.

ii

(after Lessing)

An ostrich boomed, *I wanna fly!*
And raced as fast as he could
Across the plain, beneath the sky —
The fastest of any bird.

He ran so hard he lost his breath:
With one last desperate bound
He briefly soared to a hero's death
And smashed into the ground.

iii

A frog swam into a shallow pool
And fell asleep. The sun
Heated the lakeside slowly. *Fool!*

An adder hissed: *No fun*
For me, though, if you don't survive! –
And slept as well. The lake
Grew hotter. The frog awoke – and lived.
An eagle ate the snake.

iv

   (after Lessing)

Bones, skin and putrid flesh were all
Of a hero's famous war-horse
That remained, after a fatal fall,
While Nature ran her course.

A swarm of wasps had made their nest
Inside this rotting beast –
Whose glorious history was their boast,
Whose carcass their fixed feast.

v

   (Heine, "Ein Fichtenbaum steht einsam")

In the North a lonely fir-tree
On a barren mountain height
Slumbers, benumbed by blankets
Of ice-and-snowy white.

He dreams of a sunlit palm-tree
In the farthest East of all –
Where she grieves, alone and silent
On a scorching rocky wall.

vi

    (after Lessing)

Beneath a massive oak-tree, a pig –
Eyes glued to the leaf-strewn ground –
Ate acorn after acorn. Big
And smart – though muddy – he grubbed all round.

Tall branches waved in the autumn wind:
Ungrateful brute, hissed the tree.
The pig kept munching, grunted, grinned:
You didn't drop 'em for me!

vii

A lion, enraged with his partner, a wolf,
For having the nerve to divide
Their prey in equal parts, engulfed
His head with a roar. The wolf died.

Their fellow-hunter, a fox, to appease
His Highness, begged to suggest
He eat what he liked. The lion, pleased,
Allowed him to feast on the rest.

viii

A raven found a lump of cheese
And perched with it in her beak
On a branch. A dog-fox wheedled, *Please,
Mrs Crow, you look so sleek –*

*With your beak so strong and pointed – won't
You sing for me – I know
You can, o Queen of the Birds – I can't
Wait for a song or two…*

    *

The fox's wife spoke next. The serene
Raven still held her lump
Of Cheddar. *Call yourself a Queen?*
She sneered. *You sad old frump!...*

But the raven paid no serious heed
To the praise or blame of such
Sly (self-) deceivers – who shortly agreed
They'd never liked cheese much.

ix

A lion had caught a hare when a stag
Ran by. The hare cried, *Lunch,
Your Majesty! – A BIGGER bag
Of bones for you to crunch!!*

– *Don't move,* the lion growled – and followed
The fleet-footed stag. Hares hide
With ease. The greedy lion swallowed
Nothing that day but his pride.

x

A bull dropped so much dung on a field
The mice who lived there too
Thought up a plan to try and shield
Their holes from his pats of poo:

When he raised his tail, one ran out and bit
His nose – ran in – repeated
The process. The roaring bull, plus bullshit,
Angrily – helplessly – retreated.

xi

A badly treated slave complained
To Aesop that his master
Beat him for nothing. Aesop explained
That blows would rain the faster
If he *did* something, such as try
To run away. Blows rained
On the slave as before: "It's do or die,"
He decided. Ventured. And gained.

xii

(after Tommaso da Celano)

St Francis praised a flock of birds
For joyfully praising their Maker
In beautiful song, as he with words:
"Gratitude turns a taker
Into an open-hearted giver,
My sisters, who neither sow
Nor reap – praise, praise the wind and weather,
And all things here below!

Be praised, with all Your creatures, Lord:
We thank You for our Mother the Earth
Who supports and feeds us, bringing forth
Her berries and fruits, her trees and grass.

Be praised for Brother Wind – for the air
And constantly changing weather,
Cloudy and cool or soft and fair! –
Where all things change and pass.

Opus 1, No. 3: Interpretations

O God, I could be bounded in a nutshell and count myself a king of infinite space – were it not that I have bad dreams.
　　　　　　　Hamlet II.ii.254–256

*Man is the only being by whom a destruction can be accomplished…
[Storms] do not destroy … they merely modify the distribution of masses of beings. After the storm there is something else. [But] to posit otherness there must be a witness who can retain the past in some manner and compare it to the present in the form of no longer. In the absence of this witness there is being after as before the storm – that is all.*
　　Sartre, *Being and Nothingness*, I.1.II ('Negations')

1 HAMLET IN ENGLAND

"Polonius: *What do you read, my lord?*
Hamlet: *Words, words, words.*
Polonius: *What is the matter, my lord?*
Hamlet: *Between who?*"

In other versions of the legend than Shakespeare's, Hamlet reaches England, whose king (according to his uncle's plan) is to put him to death. But Hamlet rewrites his retainers' letters, requesting that the bearers be executed. The rewritten letters also propose that Hamlet should marry the king of England's daughter. And this marriage takes place. After a year Hamlet returns to Denmark and avenges what he is by now convinced was his father's murder. He explains and justifies himself to the people, who acclaim him king.

In the following version, Hamlet has left the government of the country in the hands of Laeries, with whom he has become reconciled, and has returned with his wife and two-year-old daughter to England… He sits at his writing desk in his study, looking out through its open window into a garden of fruit-trees and roses:

Still out of joint
My thoughts withdraw
Sometimes for hours
To Elsinore.

The foolish people
And cloud-capped towers
Of that solid castle
Were a prison to me

Whose confines, wards
And dungeons weren't real
But still make me feel
Like some sort of vassal,
Bounded, unfree…

I disappoint
My father-in-law.
The English expect
Action. But I
Too often see
In my mind's eye
The ghosts of that place –

My uncle's face
Like a weathercock

Which ambitious minions
Hoping to flatter
Would timidly inspect
Before daring to utter
Their considered opinions.

Whoever spoke
Would conduct an inspection
Of the wind's direction
Pretty precisely

For fear the old
Bear, Boreas,
Might snort at them
Not very nicely.

In fact the cleverest
Kept quite mum:
A smiling echo
In that court distorted
With malice aforethought
Each word or sigh
Or hopeless cry
That it reported.

Down in the orchard
Where my father died,
Unweeded, grown
To seed, there stood
A fountain, ornamented
With sphinxes, whose stone
Was always dry
Except for when I
Had vented

My feelings. How
I curse that place!
The bitter tears,
The bitterer blood!
And the venomous brood

Of eavesdropping rats
And adders which crept
Into every hide-out
Where I inwardly wept
Or raged and cried out…

– I see them now
At my uncle's face,
But they take the forms
Of maggots and worms.

He's dead and gone.
So why these fears
With no real object?
Or am *I* their subject?
It's two whole years

Since the poison made
Him swell up and cry
And beg to be killed.

I watched him die.
I wasn't afraid
To feel fulfilled.

His life was a blight
On any beauty.
– Surely I was right
About my duty?

In that rank garden
Where my father died
He begged my pardon,
But I denied
Him the comfort. Instead,
I didn't care if I sinned:
As he suffered, I grinned
Where I used to squat
And try to hide!
I had howled and cried
In that filthy spot:
I had wished I was dead,
That my flesh would melt

Like a thing of nothing –

As a nightingale
Cannot nest, cannot sing
Where roses rot.

My curse on that garden!
On the places I'd felt
Afraid of ghosts
By *day* – when the light
Itself seemed blighted –
Heavy with curses,
Haunted, benighted.

And how weary and stale,
The air had smelt.

The ghost that came,
Although it seemed
A paternal Samson
To my uncle's lecherous
Solomon, harrowed
My heart with fear –
And my mind with doubt:

As if I'd dreamed
Them its words became
Unreal and treacherous,
My guilt in borrowed
Glory. It seemed –
And seems – to me
That with bloated words –
Like "nightmare" or "history" –
And pictures we

From inside out

Conceal our sin
From ourselves and from grace:

Unctuous, but blistery,
We film and skin
The ulcerous place,

Interpreting words
And pictures which
Interpret words
And pictures which
Interpret "things".

The corruption within
Infects unseen,

And how or why
Things seem to mean
Something – or nothing –
Had better remain

(As it always will,
While words have wings
Of nothing but breath
And pictures are seen
By mortal eyes)

Even to the wise
A mystery…

What's realest is death,

From which we flee
By other lies…

But who could express
This in words any finer
Than those of Heine? –
Let me see, let me see –
"And then a spookiness…"
How does that stanza begin?
Ah, yes. With "Then a green…":

"Then a green spookiness would grin
At me – seem cruelly to be scoffing –
While out of a squat yew-tree 'd come
A death-like moaning, gasping, coughing.

"Escaping down the avenue
To where the terrace rose to meet me,

*I'd watch the North Sea's flood-tide waves
Crash on the rocks as if to greet me.*

*"And there you could gaze far out to sea.
Often I stood there wildly dreaming.
The sea of troubles in my breast
Was also foaming, storming, screaming!*

*"The screaming, storming, foaming in
My breast had surged up no less proudly
But had become as powerless as
The waves the rocks smashed up so loudly.*

*"With envious eyes I watched the ships
Sail off to better, happier lands!
But that damned castle held me fast,
Although I cursed its bitter bonds."*

— As if to say,
In other words — words — words:
How much do we *see*
With envious eyes,
Let alone *know*
Objectively,
In a world of lies —
Our own and others',
Our father's brother's,
Our very mother's?...

For all I can tell
Of *it* from *me*,
I might as well
Be a lonely tree
On some Northern height
(As Heine said
In another rhyme),
Benumbed and white
In the mist and snow:

Such things only seem,
But the thought returns
To trouble me still
Of a distant palm…

Where do such thoughts
Originate? –
Ought-nots and oughts,
What to love, what to hate?

Am I awake?
Or do I dream –

Half-alive, or half-dead,
On my barren hill?...

Does this palm in the East
Of my mind only mock?

She probably burns
On a wall of rock,
Grieving, alone.

Does she sing, or groan?
(O the green willow)
Or merely ache –
Grow old – and yellow?...

Lost in the maze
Of my mind for days –
The forking paths
Of what ought I to do,
Or *say* at least –

How should I make
A decision to go,
Or not to go? –
As, then, to be
Or not? How free
Are our in/decisions,
Our revised revisions?

My wife delays
Our departure. Her father
Worries – would rather
She stayed. And so
She stays – and stays...

Was the play the thing?
I wish I knew.

My daughter plays
By the garden swing.

"It's *my* turn," she says.
But if fair is fair
At two years old,
And another's fair
Is another thing,
And your point of view
Gets tumbled and rolled
And sat on, who
Would not run away crying?

– "I want it," she says,
With a tearful look,
As she tries to bite
The fruit in her book.

"That's blue," she says
Of a red cascade
Of rose-petals. But,
At the age of two
(And later?) who
Can call a shade
A shade?

– She cannot know
How ill all's here
About my heart.

She weeps like a smile –
And sheds a smile
Like a leaf or a tear!

Her laugh is a cry,
Which helps me defy
The infected part
Played by the voice
Of guilt or fear…
Will she help us make

A decision to go?

The longer we stay
The weaker I grow.

What *now* of self-slaughter?

When sparrows fall,
It's because they fly.

But they're guiltless of choice,

Whereas you and I,
Must decide to take

Another breath,
Another way:

O my wife,
O my daughter,
The readiness is all –
For death,
For life!

If it be now
It's not to come.
If it be not
To come, it will
Be now. If it
Be not now, yet
It will come. Let
Be.

2 A BOHEMIAN PAINTER LOOKS HIMSELF IN THE EYE

"Suppose I try to be your mirror"
— Sartre, *In Camera* (1944)

i 'Who Do You Think *You* Are?'

The painter doffs his floppy hat
And (discreetly) dons a businessman's.
Why should he look
Like this or like that? —
The geo-physicist's wife along the road,
Doing a doctorate in philosophy, wears
The latest student fashions, believes
In the 'unification' of society.
To explain this she refers
To mythemes, semes and phemes,
Dicent-symbol-legisigns,
Rhematic-indexical-sinsigns and
Icons. The painter, though, is racking
His mind with conflicting modes
Of that or this — of wrong or right —
Of right or left — white/black, black/white —
Around him and within him,
Which bedazzle and bedim him
Until his head is reeling
As if he were drunk or mad.
How do you think in colour, when your soul
Is giddy with conflict? Or choose your style,
For bad or good — for good or bad —
From who can tell how many ways
Of seeing / thinking / feeling?
Your role
Is also yours to choose.
The cameras smile.
And though we shan't all miss what we lose,
Some fail to recognize
Their face / their eyes
In mirrors they fear are cracking
Or starting to fall to bits —
And turn in terror from that vision

Where nothing combines or fits –
Where your feelings contradict your considered opinion –
And your opinions and your feelings somehow differ
When the matter concerns yourself from when it concerns
Your wife – your family – social circle – the political
Set-up in the land you happen to live in –
Your religious world, your business world –

ii   'If You See, You're Seen' – Four Surreal Quatrains

The camera bares omnivorous teeth:
Its 'seems' is all we have of 'is'.
A stranger's head, concealed beneath
The hood, has neither ears nor eyes.

I snap my camera back at him:
We pose before each other lest
With crazy intellectual zest
Some hog-like boor should trample the gem

Which skinny, camera-snouted pigs –
And fat pink prudent slotted ones
With identical specs, false teeth and wigs –
Competing with pearl-handled guns,

Shoot to protect – the brittle glass,
With many, many facets,
Which some have glimpsed on the steel grass
In shiny, tiny bits.

iii   Visiting The Mad – Twelve Sketches *à la japonaise*

  Ignored by these viewers,
A frustrated would-be ace
  Screws up Wimbledon

    .

Mixed has-beens (horny
And highly-strung as catgut)
  Lick or chew the mike

     .

Flashers and nymphos
Sit slamming lonely foreheads
  In their distant cells

     .

Now in the corner
Some madman's climbing Everest —
  By himself, of course

     .

Vexed by empty shelves,
Poets CRY. For attention.
  By hook or by crook

     .

Is this a mad-house,
Mountain, book-shop, office-block —
  Or run-down brothel

          ?

On, on! In on. Up
On. On up, on up, on up,
  Up, UP! Down. And out

     .

If we can't get no
Satisfaction, we don't want
  No satisfaction

     .

Nerves knotted, wired to
The gabbling set, millions lust
For gold and silver

.

Unattainable
Rewards! Even vengeance is
Unattainable

.

You can't win, can you?
But what if you're punished for
Losing? Here they know

.

Break things till a nurse
Straps you howling to a post!
Smash your own face up.

3 A KING AND NOT A KING

"Although democratic then
The frogs begged a royal yoke"
– La Fontaine, *Fables* III, 4

"Whenever history makes her move she catches us unawares… Since the general purpose
of society is the safety of its members, it should first postulate the total arbitrariness of history,
and the limited value of any recorded negative experience. Second, it should postulate that,
although its institutions will strive to obtain the greatest measure of safety, this very quest for
stability and security effectively turns society into a sitting duck. And third, if you don't want to
become a target, you should move."
– Joseph Brodsky, *Profile of Clio*

                    The frogs interpreted
                    Their world so anxiously
                    That thousands now are dead
Who might have lived and croaked in peace beneath a moonlit sky.
But neither sun- nor moon-light could dispel their fear of why
The darkness kept returning, while their dread
                    Of death or danger made some freeze
                    In panic, others seek distraction
                    In meaningless activities –
                    Much movement, little action…
Until, afraid – or so it seemed – of poverty, of hunger,
One clan indulged in greed, self-interest, anger,
                    And strove to dominate the others,
Who might have swum elsewhere (the lakeland bogs were endless)
But stood up for their ranine rights: *All frogs are brothers –*
So what about the poor and sick, the retarded, lame and friendless?
                    We weak are many, the strong are few:
                    We need a king to see that all
                    Are fairly treated. Ah, but who
Will take upon himself so hard and thankless a role?
The wise are sure to abstain, but heaven protect us from a fool!
Whereon they asked their Frog-god what to do:
That is, they prayed – but nothing happened. Then,
One day a rotten bough from high in a tree
                    Came crashing down into their fen
                    With an almighty splash, which they
Took as a sign from God that this, their wished-for king,
                    Would stand no nonsense. All the frogs
Were truly terrified. And hid in pools, ponds, lakes and bogs

                Until the following spring
When, feeling somewhat braver, they emerged. Till one of the greedy,
Observing from the rushes how their king did literally nothing,
            Dared to approach him – hopped on top –
            And found he was no living frog
Of any sort, but an unmoving, water-logged 'King Log',
On whom the other members of the clan now also hop,
Soon to be followed by thousands of the needy…
Order restored at last, they start to think
            There must have been some mistake,
            But whose? Some, dwelling in bog and lake,
            Suspected a tasteless joke
            On the part of their cousins, the tree-frogs…
            Others, mud-stirrers, caused a stink
            By claiming this 'king' was no king but a fake
            Who'd failed to survive the winter… Or
            (Since all of the more
Highly developed species had their own king or queen)
Could it – the log – be a test, perhaps, of their faith
            In Frog their Father?… Worried to death
By this last eventuality, the leaders of the needy –
            On behalf of all free frogs
            (Including the greedy) –
Soon begged forgiveness of Him who'd created them in His image
            For their sacrilegious misbehaviour.
            Moreover, regarding their humble wish
            For an earthly (or rather 'aquatic') king –
            Whether frog, fowl or fish –
            To be their saviour
By guiding and ruling all, His will of course be done,
But might they be sent another, more active monarch – one
Who'd *tell* them what to do and how to live?
How not to take from others, how to share – or even give…
And so they prayed again, and nothing happened. Then,
One day the tranquil surface of the largest lake
Was troubled by the lazy coils of a voracious water-snake.
            – Was *this* their king?! A desperate scrimmage
            To escape ensued – for many in vain,
            And for more and more as time went on.
The needy asked themselves what they had done
To bring down such a curse upon their race. They might have swum
            Elsewhere again. But leaving home
            Meant crossing the great unknown

     Of which they'd always feared the worst –
     And so they stayed. Until, again,
The bravest of the greedy – this time a delegation –
Observing how their king had breakfasted fit to burst,
     Approached him with trepidation
     And reverently inquired
     As to whence and why he'd come –
And why he *ate* his subjects with such calm
Persistence. His snout and tongue being half-immersed,
     His sibilous sussuration –
They s-s-said you were s-s-seeking a king – was hard to hear.
     Its import, though, was clear.
– *But not a king like you!* their leader blurted, vexed.
The enormous, unblinking water-snake suspired,
Well, if that's-s-s how you s-s-see it, s-s-sir, I'd better eat you firs-s-st –
     You other trouble-makers-s-s nex-x-xt.
From which they learned to welcome their new ruler – in the hope
He'd treat them better. Or, disgusted with the narrow scope
Of every meal – as well as being required
By his size to eat so much – depart in peace. Or even die
     One wintry night, or summer's day…

It didn't work. The frogs interpreted
     His words / their world so fearfully
     That many thousands now are dead
Who might have lived beneath another sky…

– They had no rights; there was no god, no king; they were not cursed,
     Except by what they foolishly desired:
     Snakes eat frogs anyway.

4 PICASSO'S CHILDREN. *OR:* WAYS OF SEEING / WAYS OF SAYING

"Probably I don't have a style. As often as not, style is something that ties an artist down to the same way of seeing, to the same technique, the same formulations… You recognize it at once, but it's always the same suit of clothes… As for myself, I hit out too wildly, am too much of a vagabond. You see me here but already I've changed and am somewhere else. I'm never tied down. That's why I don't have a style." – Picasso

1895–1897

A barefoot girl, wearing a plain red dress,
Plays queen on a barren patch of dusty ground.
Behind her the dark and threatening emptiness
Could panic her soft eyes with one big bound.

And so a feverish woman lies in bed
Nursed by an elderly doctor and young nun,
Who holds her child. Yet when her mother's dead,
Will she – and will her children – then live on

In unassertive innocent affirmation? –
Like Pablo's sister, kneeling dressed in white
At First Communion. Her parents' resignation
Highlights her hope. But in the encroaching night

Is she too young – are they too old – to learn
Two candles dead means two are left to burn?

1901

After Picasso's impotent friend
Had blown out his brains,
                              the heartless spring
Arrived with its usual flurry and fling
Of seed and sunshine.
                      A bitter end,
But artists / children keep repeating
The old made new.

                        A girl with a bowl
Concentrates heart and guts and soul
On what she stands at the table eating.

Another cuddles a dove.
                        She sends
A sweet demanding look of the sort
No well-trained parent would wish to refuse.
But though she performs
                        and the other blends
Into the background, lost in thought,

How freely do children / artists choose?

1902–1906

Clasping her thin blue child, a mother waits
On a dismal shore for an ominous empty boat
To fetch them. The child absorbs her sickly whites
But not the tiny red of the flower she's brought.
And even the family of tumblers, left behind
Or waiting, oppress the children, like the thumb
And little finger of a hopeless hand
Raised in the wasteland. But who oppresses *them?*...

Across that dusty ground a short time after
The son comes naked, leading a bright grey horse.
At home, the departed tumblers' drum becomes
A makeshift table. His sister's abandoned flowers
Blush in a vase. And their youngest brother's laughter
Helps free his pick-a-backed body's growing force.

1923–1924 / 1954

" 'Now, Kitty,' said Alice, 'let's consider who it was
that dreamed it all.' "

To the upside-down world it was Pablo who said
"I've a harlequin-suit on, and eyes in my head:
Let all back-to-front creatures, whoever they be,
Come and pose for Queen Olga, Pablito and me."

"Come take up your cameras as quick as you can
Before he becomes a wild Minotaur man –
Or changes his mind or his clothes or his wife!
And let's all wish King Pablo a very long life!"

"O arse-licking crawlers," said Pablo, "draw near:
It's an honour to meet you, a favour to hear!
Your creeping-and-crawling 's a pleasure to see
For Claude and Paloma, Queen Françoise and me."

*

And as children make-believe their roles are real,

        He'd substitute
           For "harlequin-suit"

Gentleman's wig –
   Blue Period coat –
Bright red cravat
(Absurdly big) –
   Catalan hat –

Braque's uniform –
   Prize-fighter's shorts –
Sporran and kilt
(Absurdly warm) –
   Etc. –

To fit the ways we see and think and feel.

1934–1937

Guided towards his Apollonian self
By a girl he trusts, who cuddles a soft white dove,
The Minotaur heaves his huge blind heavy head
To the starry sky in search of innocent love.

And now he's in danger. A screaming, flailing mare
Could stamp him to death.
                              Unless the living light
Of the girl's small candle leads him to a ladder
And both escape
                to watch the final fight
Of hooves with horns
                      from the dove-cote above…

(Guernica)

But beneath this eye-bulb,

                the child is dead – the bull
            Alive – the horse
            still screaming…

                        Asked by a Nazi
"Did you do that?" he answered, "Yes. And *you* did."

– Though long before Picasso artists chose

To cultivate
        the wastes
                where nothing grows.

1656 / 1957

(Self-Portrait as a Gentleman-in-Waiting)

Trying to believe
                he's bigger than
                              the maids-
And ladies-in-waiting,
                the Infanta Margarita Maria
And the docile dog being kicked by an attendant midget,

The thin blue painter,
                        holding his palette and brushes,
Only succeeds in looking unsure of himself,
As if, in his inmost thoughts,
                            he wished he could blend —
As he seems to do —
                into the blues of the background.

His studio imprisons him.
                      Are the hooks in the ceiling
For lights?
          His subjects — the King and Queen —
Are only seen
        in a mirror
                on the far wall
                          behind him,
So that he and the children look
                in our direction.
And I ask
      myself:
            Are artists still nothing but minions,

Like gentlemen-in-waiting
                long ago —
Or

    is   who
    it   see
    only them
    I   so?

1973–1998–????

Children were not a danger. Being a child
In so many ways himself, he never snarled
At them again. Or cubed them into cold
And distant forms. Instead, while they revealed

A fresh new way of looking, he painted and lolled
In their mothers' and others' arms. Playful, self-willed,
When life as moulded by each body dulled
He left and began again, re-making the world

From a fresh new model, aesthetically impelled
To demonstrate the ways in which he ruled
The space between ourselves and the endless, unspoiled
Flux of what really happens. It never failed

For him. But abandoned mothers and children sprawled
To bitter ends. Art was his only child.

(1998)

5   THIRTY-NINE SONGS *(ca. 1250 / 2002)*

"Art can proceed only from a purely anonymous centre."
– Rainer Maria Rilke, *Letter to 'R.S.' (22 November, 1920)*

"Because I need a passionate syntax for passionate subject-matter I compel myself to accept those traditional metres that have developed with the language… All that is personal soon rots, it must be packed in ice or salt… If I wrote of personal love or sorrow in free verse or in any rhythm that left it unchanged amid all its accidence, I would be full of self-contempt because of my egotism and indiscretion, and foresee the boredom of my reader. I must choose a traditional stanza, even what I alter must seem traditional… Talk to me of originality and I will turn on you with rage. I am a crowd, I am a lonely man, I am nothing. Ancient salt is best packing."
– W.B. Yeats, *A General Introduction to My Work* (1937)

"Go, song, surely thou mayest
Whither it please thee
For so art thou ornate that thy reasons
Shall be praised from thy understanders,
With others hast thou no will to make company."
– Ezra Pound, *Canto XXXVI*

i

Sing, cuckoo, sing,
Merrily sing *cuckoo!*

Sing now spring is coming in,
Sing loudly now *cuckoo!*

Trees are blowing, leas growing,
Green is the woodland now.

Sing, cuckoo, sing,
Now sing, *cuckoo, cuckoo!*

Loudly ewes bleat for their lambs –
Cows, for calves, moo,

Bucks are rutting, bullocks snorting,
Merrily sing *cuckoo!*

You
Sing so well, cuckoo:

Mad bird, don't caw or coo,
Just cuckoo *cuckoo!* cuckoo.

ii

Birds flit through thrashing trees,
Fish flash through the dark flood.
And I? go nowhere. Mad,
I burn and then I freeze
For the best of flesh – bone – blood.

iii

Mérry life ís while summer lasts
    With birds in song.
Now, though, autumn's windy blasts
    Are cold and strong.
Black is the night, alas! and long,
    When hé who's been wronged
Suffers and mourns and fasts.

iv

When nightingales sing
The woods grow green:
Grass, leaves and blossom spring,
And mý poor heart has been
Skewered in April
As by a spear so keen
I bleed all night, all day,
Suffering súch sharp pain,

Dear love, that if this song
Should ever reach your ear,

Listen: I've loved so much, so long,
That Í can love no more:
Love-sick, I too grow green!
But a kiss alone from your
Sweet mouth might shut *my* mouth –
At best, effect a cure.

v

The shadowy air of April
Is cold and dead
Still,

The red and gold is still
In your hair.

But never still the same
Young flame in your face:

Sap-like, flame will still
Flare – shadows run –

And your head still turn – swing
Your hair in the sun,

Till it burn sun-red,
Sun-gold.

The shadowy air of April
Is cold and dead
Still –

And the spring is still
In your tread.

vi

Through raging storms
The wordless, elated stillness
Of the rose-bush grows
From root to shoot
To stem to blood-
red rose-bud. Forms
Its summer aroma. Waits
Until the rains go
And the sun loom
For its full-blooded, un-
budded, full-bodied
BLOOM
To come – to breathe – to blow –

vii

I dreamt the day was dawning
And you and I must part
And each go home. The morning
Got off to a bad start.

In my dream you'd slept, a white-gowned queen,
In a garden of snow-white roses – green
With hedges, lawns, sweet-scented flowers –
And there I'd sat for hours and hours
Until you woke and plucked a rose:

You'd dreamt the day was dawning
And you and I must part
And each go home. The morning
Got off to a sad start.

In your dream was another garden, green
With trees and hedges. A white-gowned queen,
You'd slept among sweet-scented flowers.
And there I'd sat for hours and hours –
Until you woke and plucked a rose.

– I dreamt the day was dawning
And you and I must part
And each go home…
                         But the morning
Woke us at last, sweetheart.

Which made a better start.

viii

Twigs bud in May:
Love-sick, I hardly sleep
By night or day.

To drive my cares away
And greet the spring,
I walked in the forest yesterday
And heard one sing:
"May the clod cling
To him! And may his thing
Wither away!"

When I heard these merry words repeated,
I hurried there,
And found her in an orchard, seated
With flowers in her hair
Under a pear:
"My girl, what's your sweet song about?"
With a pretty pout,

She sang in her merry way
Words pert and few:
"My lover promised me
That he'd be true,
But now he has a new
Mistress. I'll make him rue
The day today!"

ix

A rich old miller's only daughter
  Was wooed by rich young men:
When her father asked her, *Which?* she replied
  She'd marry no one.

Money and youth were nothing: only
  A mouth of solid gold,
She declared, would kiss her mouth. All flesh
  Was mortal mould.

A sly magician heard of this,
  Who lay on the village green.
He conjured from an old horse-bone
  A horse for a queen.

He pricked and pranced the horse outside
  Her father's gates on the grass,
Like an angel bearing gifts of gold.
  A pricker he was.

Her father's servants showed this prince
  Or prancer into the hall.
They tried to lock his magic horse
  In a wooden stall.

The summer evening passed, night fell.
  To bed they went, these two.
Sweetly the night passed. Sky-larks sang –
  Also the cuckoo.

— Where are you all, my women and men?
  Why don't you come to me,
And open the windows of my tower,
  So I can see?

When they opened the windows of her tower
  She saw neither duke nor earl.
The magician took the feeble form
  Of a blear-eyed churl.

Alas! she said. Her servants led him
    To a hanging tree on a hill.
As he dropped he leered, and took the form
    Of a sack of meal.

The dust fell in her eyes. And now
    She's blear-eyed, too… Beguiled
By gold-lust, any girl might end
    Like this rich man's child.

x

The girl I love has gone away –
Which makes no sense to me.

I cannot follow, must stay
At home – not bound, not free.

She's taken my heart – to have and hold
Far over land and sea,

With half its secret love untold:
Song, tell it her secretly.

xi

– My girl, your lovely rose-red mouth
Will soon be pale. No boring wife,
With boys you've danced away your youth:
With me you'll dance away your life.

            *

Help, help! Though I don't want to die,
Life's somehow not much fun any more.
Even the Dance of Death's a bore,
Forget it. And so, *Goodbye, goodbye…*

xii

"My dear, when your husband's away from home,
    Can I be so bold
And knock at your bedroom window
    When nights are long and cold?
And will you open your window
    When nights are cold and wet,
And let me lie in your husband's place?
    Will you do that?"

– "Young man, if you'll be so kind,
    When my husband's away from home,
As to knock at my bedroom window,
    When I am all alone,
And lie in my husband's place,
    I'll tell you what:
He lies there five whole times in a night.
    Will *you* do that?"

xiii

– Where are you off to now, my lad?
I'll show you a path which leads elsewhere,
To a private place. Though I'm afraid
Lots of laddish lovers lie there...

                *

Wining and dining and having it off in
Bordellos run by fat madames,
My life was nothing but fun and games…
I never dreamt I'd fill a coffin…

xiv

My head ached fit to burst last night,
So that when I sat down to write
   Today the migraine caused such pain –
   Piercing my brow and spearing my brain –
That I can scarcely look at light.

The other morning after Mass
I wrote some verses more or less,
   But the *mots justes* I tried to find
   Were lost at the back of my sleepless mind
In dreary dullness and distress.

Quite often I get out of bed
With my courage still asleep or half-dead.
   No laughter, music, fun and games,
   No prancing gents or dancing dames
Can drive the night out of my head.

I'd like to find in this unstable
World one thought or vision able
   To make a bed to lie or die on.
   But the only thing men can rely on
Is that all things are unreliable.

Yesterday's flowers are scattered by showers:
After every joy come cares.
   Maudlin tonight and gay tomorrow:
   But after comfort sorrow.
Such is this world and always was.

xv

Western wind, when will you blow,
    And when the small rains rain?

— Christ, if my love
    Were in my arms

And I
    In my bed again!

xvi

— *Come, noble warrior, sheathe your sword,*
And screw, if you want to save your face,
Your courage to the sticking place.
Death is the hero's last reward.

          *

I terrified my enemies,
Though armed and in harness cap-à-pie —
As death has seized and rattled *me*,
Grimly forcing me to my knees.

xvii

— *With ladies you have danced, proud Duke,*
And had them come and had them go.
The dead may make you want to puke,
But take their hands and say hello.

          *

Dammit, must I be off so quickly
And leave land, friends, wife, children, fame
Behind, until I look the same
As these — as thin and sickly?

xviii

— Mother, oh mother, I can't get my breath,
Give me some bread, I'm starving to death.
"Be brave and don't cry now, my little man,
Tomorrow we'll sow as fast as we can."

    And when they'd sowed the corn,
    The child was still forlorn.,

— Mother, oh mother, I can't get my breath,
Give me some bread, I'm starving to death.
"Don't cry now, have patience, my little man,
We're cutting the corn as fast as we can."

    And when they'd cut the corn,
    The child was still forlorn.

— Mother, oh mother, I can't get my breath,
Give me some bread, I'm starving to death.
"Be patient, be patient, my little man,
We're threshing the corn as fast as we can."

    And when they'd threshed the corn,
    The child was still forlorn.

— Mother, oh mother, I can't get my breath,
Give me some bread, I'm starving to death.
"Be patient and wait now, my little man,
We're grinding the corn as fast as we can."

    And when they'd ground the corn,
    The child was still forlorn.

— Mother, oh mother, I can't get my breath,
Give me some bread, I'm starving to death.
"Wait, oh wait, my little man,
We're baking the bread as fast as we can."

    But when they'd baked the bread,
    The child was dead.

xix

What sort of thing
Is a year with no spring,
A bird that can't sing,
A bell that won't ring?

– The same sort of stuff
As a child that can't laugh,
A riff that won't raff,
A stiff with a staff.

xx

When my eyes mist
And ears hiss,

When my nose feels cold
And tongue grows mould,

When my chops go slack,
Lips black,

Mouth grins,
Spittle runs,

Hair's in tatters,
Heart pitter-patters,

Hands tremble,
Feet stumble –

Too late! too late!
With the hearse at the gate:

I can't flit – but will float,
As if on a boat,

From bed to stair
And out the front door

To where, by our gate,
A few mourners wait.

From there I'll be carried
To church to be buried

With a prayer – get put
In a hole, mouth shut

With earth. A rose
Is planted. My nose

Won't smell its root.
But I don't give a hoot.

Nor will I care
For life up there.

xxi

When I consider how this life
Is always changing: peace and strife,
Sorrow and joy – no sort of rest
Or calm – I think, when cares are rife,
To take things easy is the best.

Considering, too, that the power and glory
Of this great world will soon be history,
When all seems threatened or lost
Why seek revenge – rant, rave – feel sorry?
To take things easy is the best.

Life's a mere flash in the blind eye
Of nothingness. I think the more we
Rage or lose heart when attacked / oppressed,
The more we suffer, the sooner die.
To take things easy is the best.

Whoever schemes or fights to win
Gains, in the end, the wages of sin:
No one and nothing on earth can last.

So live / let live. Through thick and thin,
To take things easy is the best.

xxii

On the sands a girl stood sighing,
Wearing an anxious frown.
It almost had her crying
To see the sun go down.

I hope (my dear) it won't bore you,
But you really shouldn't mind:
The sun goes down before you –
And comes back up behind.

xxiii

One girl marries for money,
One for a handsome face,
A third for a taste of honey,
A fourth on Mama's advice.

A fifth can't live by herself,
A sixth was left on the shelf.
The seventh and eighth are too dim
To know why him / not him.

xxiv

"Rosemary and thyme
Grow in our garden.
Mother, give me a man –
I can't wait any longer!"

– "My daughter, sour's not sweet:
No labourer with flat feet!
But a gent from the city –
And rich, not just pretty…"

xxv

By the long slow river's pebbles and ooze,
I helped a girl put on – when she told me –
Firstly her stockings, then her shoes.
But in the end she fooled me…

If Í'd known then what I know now,
I'd have banged her belly full.
For that, you see, would have been how
To lead her up the aisle.

xxvi

The bimbambolical church is ringing
    With a bimbambolical row!
A bimbambolical ox has married
    A bimbambolical cow.
Her bimbambolical mother is cooking
    A bimbambolical treat,
Which the bimbambolical children are sticking
    Their fingers in to eat.

xxvii

Your rose-red cheeks are wan, my girl,
    As pale and green as the grass.
Your apron hides a bun, my girl –
    It's shorter but not less…

    Oh you've been sleeping wrong, my girl,
        You've been sleeping all wrong –
    Been sleeping in an unquiet bed
        With an unquiet man.

You've let the donkey over the dyke
    And hé's been in the corn;
The greens you eat before you sleep
    Are vomited by dawn.

Over the hills you'd stride, my girl,
    And through the woods have sung;
But stealing honey from a hive,
    Young lady, you've been stung.

    Oh you've been sleeping wrong, my girl,
        You've been sleeping all wrong –
    Been sleeping in an unquiet bed
        With an unquiet man.

xxviii

The summer night was dark – no moon
    Was in the gloomy sky.
The only stars that could be seen
    Peeped from her dark-blue eye
When, at her father's door, I knocked,
    Where I had often been:
Dressed only in her short white smock,
    She upped and let me in.

Locked now in one another's arms,
    She trembled where we stood.
Our hearts being close, her breasts' full forms
    Were warm with pumping blood
Until, without a word, the thing
    I thought I'd have to win
Was round my finger like a ring:
    I upped – she let me in.

She let me in and out all night:
    I'd known no greater joy
Than out and in and in and out,
    And on and on till day
When she, now melting with delight,
    Told me to come again
And promised each and every night
    To up and let me in.

Alas, her lovely belly grew –
    Till she sat there, sad and dull,
And I, not knowing what to do,
    Stood by her like a fool.
The tears ran down her scarlet cheeks:
    Had it not been a sin?
She rued the nights and days and weeks
    She'd upped and let me in.

But I could never leave her – on
    Her own, and in the lurch.
And soon her mother found she'd gone
    And married in a church.
Her father raged – and threw a fit…
    But now all's well again.
And our red-letter day 's the night
    She upped and let me in.

xxix

The night and the streets are still, as I go
To take a look at the house where she lived.
She left this city years ago.
But the house looks just like it did.

And a man stands, as if in my place,
Wringing his hands in constant pain.
It gives me a shock to glimpse his face:
The moon shows me myself again.

You there, my double! looking so sick,
Why do you ape the ridiculous plight
In which I was cut to the very quick
In times gone by here, night after night?

xxx

"Where have you been all winter, my son?
Where did you live and what have you done?"
– "I built a house in Heligoland."
– "That's good."
             "What's good? It was built on sand,
And a wild pig came and knocked it down."
– "That's bad."
            "What's bad? I took my gun,
And shot the pig for its skin and its meat."
– "That's good."
             "What's good? Two feet and four feet
Stole my meat in the thick of the night."
– "That's bad."
            "What's bad? I cut off their flight.
Four feet is now my friend for life,
And two feet my wife."

xxxi

Who rides so late through the night so wild?
A father with his only child.
He carries the boy in the crook of his arm;
He holds him safe, he keeps him warm.

"Why, son, do you hide your face in fear?"
– "Look, father, can't you see him there?
The Erlking with his crown and cloak?"
– "My son, that's only fog or smoke."

O sweetest child, come live with me!
We'll play together happily.
Look where bright flowers on the beach invite you!
My mother has golden clothes to delight you.

"O father, can't you hear the hiss
When the Erlking whispers his promises?"
– "Hush, hush now, child: it's only the sighing
Of the wind where the leaves are dry and dying."

Won't you take, my dainty boy, this chance?
My daughters lead our nightly dance:
They'll love and nurse you if you weep
And rock and dance and sing you to sleep.

"O father, father, can't you see
His daughters under that gloomy tree?"
– "My child, my child, as clear as day,
It's only the willows that look so grey."

I love you, I can't wait to take you;
If you won't come willingly, I'll make you!
"O father, he's taking hold of me!
The Erlking's hands are hurting me." –

The exhausted father races on;
He holds in his arms his moaning son.
He reaches home in horror and dread:
The child he holds in his arms is dead.

xxxii

I have smelt my way through every smell
In this earthly kitchen: I know full well
The taste and aftertaste of pleasure.
I have lived like a hero, without measure.
I have drunk my coffee and eaten my cake
And taken all there is to take
From the women I've kept. For better or worse,
There was silk on my back and gold in my purse.
Like the well-bred agent in a thriller,
I owned a house, I owned a villa:
I happily lay in the summer grass,
And the lucky sun shone out of my arse.
A wreath of laurels graced my brow
And scented dreams, I don't know how,
Seemed to come true – of roses, of May –
Till I revelled in roses day after day,
Lazy and drunk on the wines of the south –
And roasted pigeons flew into my mouth –
And angels descended like golden rain,
Producing bottles of champagne…

These dreams were nothing but soap-bubbles.

They burst and left me with my troubles.

xxxiii

A red-haired cooper once, called Rob,
   Was the quickest cooper on call:
He came to hoop our landlady's tub –
   And banged her buttocks against the wall.

"Cooper," she said, "have you got any money?"
   – "Nothing," said Robbie, "nothing at all."
So she took out her purse and gave him a guinea,
   For banging her buttocks against the wall.

xxxiv

There lived a widow in Cockpen,
  Will you not, can you not, let me be?
She brewed good ale for gentlemen,
  And always wagged it cheerily.

One winter evening, cold and wet,
  Will you not, can you not, let me be?
She showed a traveller to his bed,
  And wagged it wantonly.

She saw a sight below his belt,
  Will you not, can you not, let me be?
She wouldn't have missed for all the world,
  And wagged it happily.

She saw a sight above his knee,
  Will you not, can you not, let me be?
She wouldn't have missed for all the beer
  In her cellar. *And wagged it wildly:*

"Oh where do you live and what's your trade?"
  Will you not, can you not, let me be?
– "A thresher I am, for hire," he said.
  She wagged it smilingly.

"And that's my flail and working gear."
  Will you not, can you not, let me be?
– "Fine tools you've brought to serve me here,"
  She smiled. *And wagged it gleefully:*

"A barrel of ale, the best I have,"
  Will you not, can you not, let me be?
"I'd give for a long hard night with all that,"
  She said. *And wagged it tirelessly:*

"I'd sell the hair from off my tail,"
  Will you not, can you not, let me be?
"To buy our thresher such a flail,"
  And so she wagged it and wagged it.

xxxv

She often had dead flowers in her room,
Which worried him a bit.

Not that he felt offended by cut bloom
But, having cut at it,

One might expect her to provide fresh water.
Or was it flower-slaughter?

xxxvi

I don't know why things seem
Today so hopelessly sad:
An age-old story, or dream,
Is stuck in my aching head.

The wind is cool, and it wrinkles
The smoothly flowing Rhein.
The tip of the mountain twinkles
In the last of the day's sunshine.

A beautiful girl, reclining
On a steep rock up there,
With golden jewellery shining,
Combs out her golden hair.

With a golden comb she combs it
And, overpoweringly,
Sings a strange song – intones its
Echoing melody.

In his small boat a boatsman,
Nearing where rapids swirl –
Seized by wild longing – can only
Look up at the singing girl…

The river (I can't help thinking)
Swallowed the boat and the man.
And that's what, with her singing,
The Lorelei has done.

xxxvii

What lay on my eyes was darkness,
What lay on my mouth was lead.
With stiffening heart and forehead
I lay among the dead.

How long I had lain there sleeping
I can't say now for sure.
I woke – it seemed – when I heard her
Knocking at death's stone door.

"Won't you get up now, dearest?
Behold, the eternal Sun;
The dead are all arisen;
Eternal joy has begun."

– My love, I can't get up yet.
I seem to have lost my sight.
I must have cried my eyes out.
All I can see is the night.

"I'll kiss you better, dearest,
I'll kiss away your night.
I want you to see the angels
And all this heavenly light."

– My love, I can't get up yet.
Perhaps you haven't heard –
I'm bleeding from where you stabbed me
In the heart with a single word.

"I'll stroke it gently, dearest,
I'll relieve your heart of its pain.
And then it will stop bleeding
And never hurt again."

– My love, I can't get up yet,
My head is bleeding, too.
I blew my aching brains out
When I was robbed of you.

"With my curls and ringlets, dearest,
I'll stop up the hole in your head.
My hair will staunch your bleeding.
I'll heal your wounds instead."

She begged with such loving kindness,
Who could have answered no?
Like a fool, I made my body
Get up and try to go.

My clotted wounds reopened;
A flood of bleeding broke
From my rigid heart and forehead.
And then I really woke.

xxxviii

In the woods green buds are opening –
Almost girl-like – almost shy.
But the laughing sun says *Welcome,*
Spring! in the laughing sky.

Nightingale, I hear you also,
Piping sadly in a grove,
Sobbing sweet long-drawn-out phrases,
And your song is filled with love.

xxxix

Cheerful by day and lucky by night,
I've lived and loved. Some praised my songs
And others sang them. Righting wrongs,
They set hearts, bonfires, lust alight.

Summer still blooms, and yet I've brought
My harvest home already. I grieve
For all the loves and lives I must leave
Sooner than ever I'd have thought.

The hand I strummed with sinks – sends flying
A glass which, filled with foaming fizz,
I've often confidently pressed

To laughing lips. How bitter is dying!
O God, how sweet and cosy is
Life in our cosy, sweet little nest!

6   THE BRIDE'S STORY

"Benedick: Like the old tale, my lord: 'It is not so, nor 'twas not so: but indeed, God forbid it should be so!'" – Much Ado About Nothing, I.i.200–201

"The thief cometh not but to steal and to kill and to destroy. I am come that they might have life, and that they might have it more abundantly." – John X.10

Around 1800 in the township of Hanau, amid the great forests of Hessen in Central Germany, Marie Hassenpflug, then about twelve years of age, must have heard a folk-tale (or Märchen) – there was no printed version at that time – which she later told (with a number of others) to her brothers-in-law Wilhelm and Jakob Grimm, who included it as No.40 in their Kinder- und Hausmärchen (1812–14), under the title of Der Räuberbräutigam ('The Robber Bridegroom'). From the 2nd edition (1819) of the Märchen onwards Marie's tale was combined with material gathered from three other story-tellers – and in this form it is known today. 'The Robber Bridegroom' has many recorded analogues throughout Europe. The version mentioned by Benedick was already "old" in 1598; another seems to have been current in seventeenth and eighteenth century England; and Dickens claimed that the trivialized variant in ch. xv of The Uncommercial Traveller (1861) was told him by his nurse. The Grimms' tale (one of their best written) is unusually horrible – almost sacrilegious – and The Bride's Story elaborates on this:

In Hanau, on the Kinzig, there once lived
A miller, born in Frankfurt, who had thrived
Away from home – become, in fact, so rich
That of all millers on the river, which
Had more than twenty mills, he took the cake.
His daughter was a handsome girl, who'd make
A wife as staunch and sweet as any man's.
But only wealthy suitors stood a chance;
Her dad was vulgar, greedy, and a tyrant,
Which cooled the love of more than one aspirant.

At last she met by some unhappy chance
At Hanau's yearly Harvest Festival dance
A certain Captain Fox, who'd bought a house,
Left vacant in the deepest darkest Bulau's
Pathless interior – a place for fattening swine.
His father lived in Frankfurt on the Maine;
The miller knew the name: *Well-heeled*, he thought.
The property was large – just what he'd sought.
Although the rumour was he'd been a pirate,
With ready cash Fox easily acquired it.

– A much-feared robber on the Spanish Main,
A captain who'd enjoyed inflicting pain –
Or worse – on culprits… The tales, of course, were many
And gory. Fox had made a pretty penny,
Everyone knew. And brought it home with him.
His manner was forbidding, if not grim.
The miller liked him – soon he came to woo
The daughter, who was told to like him too.
A plucky girl, she was not weak or weepy.
But as for Captain Fox, she found him creepy.

Her father remonstrated. And she had
Always obeyed him until now – felt bad
About not wanting to do something he
Insisted on so energetically;
So went to ask her parish priest's advice.
The miller seldom prayed, but found it nice
That *she* did. His family had been Huguenots,
Her mother's Roman Catholics: these were pious, those
Preferred their pie on the table. Before she died,
Her mother made her promise: *Be brave, be good.*

"Honour thy father and thy mother," said
The priest – "in life, *and* after they are dead.
Unless, that is, some just impediment
Arises, which may rightfully prevent
A child from doing what it's asked to do…"
And so they were betrothed, although she knew
Something was wrong. Maria was her name:
She also pondered – "*What*, though…?" All the same,
Whenever Fox turned up to meet and greet her
She thought he looked as if he'd like to eat her.

One day he almost smiled: she'd not yet seen
The house in which she'd shortly be his queen:
"Let's have – why not? – a secret rendezvous."
He licked his lips: "Just me, the house, and you.
I'm sure you'll find it all a big surprise."
He looked at her with strange, unfeeling eyes:
"Next week is Easter week. Will Wednesday do?"
She couldn't find a reason to say no.
He'd meet her at the footbridge by the river.
Thinking of this next day, she started to quiver…

By Tuesday, though, she also thought *Why not?*
Perhaps she'd know then more exactly what
Her intuition told her was not right.
Or was she wrong about him? Awake in the night,
She was afraid of tales dismissed by day.
On Wednesday late wet snow fell, blocking the way
To the narrow bridge – on which he'd pinned a note
The night before, however, in his neat
But spiky hand... No one must see him show her
The primrose path to her pre-bridal bower...

Next day she was alone and – feeling bored –
Decided, since the snow had mostly thawed,
To find the house herself – she was sure she could,
And rode along the Kinzig into the wood...
April. The sun went in. But she could see
His note like a white bird nailed to a black tree.
– *"Be bold, ride on,"* it said: *"turn right – left – right.*
The Fox will see his fiancée home tonight!"
The clouds were grey with snow. The wind howled coldly.
But, curious now, she crossed the river boldly.

Beyond the bridge the track wound on and on
Into the ancient forest. She had gone
Much further than she'd ever been before
When all at once a house with a green door
Appeared between the trees, and the path stopped.
The door swung on its hinges. Her heart hopped.
The building was small and derelict. How could
So broken-down a place, so deep in the wood,
With cobwebbed chairs and tables, empty boxes
And rubble on the floor, be Captain Fox's?

He'd said he spent a lot of time at home.
But *here?* Impossible! Still, since she'd come,
Why not inspect the premises? Bereft
Of occupants, the house had long been left –
Sadly, she felt – to moulder and collapse.
Once full of life – a hunters' lodge, perhaps –
Only birds, bugs and spiders lodged there now
And snow blew in and dust blew out – although
The door was freshly painted. Also, pale yellow
Firelight came flickering up the steps from the cellar.

– Frightened, she gasped. But, then, crept slowly down.
A frail old woman was cooking. With a groan
She asked Maria *why*, of her own free will,
She'd come to that infernal place. She still
Had time to escape; but when *Herr Fuchs* returned…
Beneath a blackened pot a red fire burned,
Boiling what looked like joints of salted pork:
She'd seen pigs' bones and ashes round the back.
– Suddenly, though, gruff curses! frantic screaming!…
In later years, what followed seemed like dreaming

Nightmare on nightmare – which she couldn't shake
Her mind or body free of: wide awake,
She pinched her forearm purple making sure.
The old woman hid her. Lame, unwell and poor,
Unable to escape from Fox on her own,
She'd always been the cook there – had stayed on,
After the hunters left. But, small and light,
She lay in staunch Maria's lap that night
And both rode quickly home. His drunken snorting
And sated grunts accompanied their parting.

'*Once a thief…*' pre-judges – but the old saying
Made sense next day when it struck Maria, praying
In church, that Fox's tic had given her proof
Of what he'd done and might do… She was safe
And sound at home, but others lived in danger.
He was, for most young girls, a tall dark stranger
Who'd bought a house nearby not long ago.
A milkmaid and a chambermaid were two
She'd known from church, supposed to have "left the area".
But now she feared the truth was much, much scarier.

The pile of bones and ashes, the old woman told her,
Were not a pig's. At first this made her bolder:
What to do *now* about her coming marriage?
And Friday in church restored her former courage.
But then the things she'd seen made her feel sick
All over again. Was he mad? Could he be Satanic –
An Anti-Christ? Once more she asked the priest –
Who feared he was an unregenerate Beast…
Would *this* thief ever change?… Meanwhile, his duty
Must be to help maltreated – brave – shocked Beauty.

He praised her pious virtue. Every Sunday
She went to Mass, and sang in the choir. On Mondays,
Attended Morning Prayer or Evensong…
And so her spirit was willing, her flesh strong –
And so as well, he thought, still felt so shocked.
"A deeply ruthless brute. But God is not mocked:
What each man sows, that shall he also reap."
– A widely travelled padre, his flesh would creep
Still, he confided, remembering how he'd converted
To Christian rites minds almost as perverted

As Fox's – who, perhaps, had learned to kill
And cook in that same region of Brazil
Where he had laboured many years before,
Where tribes of *Tupi*, constantly at war
With one another, ate each other's leaders:
Such heroes' flesh, they thought, was sent to feed us –
And all its strength and courage, they believed,
Became one's own: whoever took received.
The weak were burned or buried – never eaten.
Their hide was used for wiping unclean feet on.

It was, in other words, an honour if
Your corpse was prized more highly than your life.
– "I was, at first, as horrified and shocked
By this as you… But then my mind unblocked –
In church, to be exact, while saying Mass.
Soon many Tupis' greatest hero was
Our Lord, whose god-like virtues were so great
That, there and then, they thought, whoever ate
The blessed bread and drank the wine became
More virtuous, strong and godlike through His name.

This turned things upside down, of course, to put
It mildly. Not instantly, or simply. But
A new commandment I give unto you…
Helped change their fundamental point of view.
And *Greater love hath no man than to lay*
His life down for his friends turned darkness to day:
He took the cup and gave it them and said
This is my blood – now and forever shed
For many. Took the bread – blessed – broke – and gave it:
To save your life is to lose it – lose it, save it.

They understood, at least, that they and He
Interpreted the world so differently
That *their* way led to never-ending Death
Whereas He breathed the everlasting breath
Of Life into the nostrils of all people.
By the time I left they'd raised a modest steeple
Out of the jungle into the deep blue
Of where they thought He'd come *from* and gone *to* –
As fearless in His dying as in His living:
Taking was now subsumed in natural giving."

– Fox, though, was neither natural nor a part
Of unresponsive things-without-a-heart.
His ruthless pirate habits seemed ingrained,
His appetites *never* to have been restrained
By thoughts of loving-kindness: he took pleasure
In taking – things / lives / bodies – without measure
Or mercy – as if, in Holy Week, to defile
Easter itself. The more you tried to unveil
A mind as dangerous, mad and bad as Fox's was,
The more it seemed inhuman, heartless, noxious…

All this being more than enough impediment
And cause why not to marry him, they spent
Saturday thinking what they should do next…
– Why *marry* at all? The answer to this vexed
Conundrum appeared to be: he'd been unable
To get her on the lodge's kitchen table
In any other way. He knew she went
To church, and that the holy sacrament
Of matrimony enjoined her to obey him…
"He'll go berserk," she groaned, "when I betray him."

– "I fear that all you'll get 's a flat denial…
He'll also find, I think, the chance to defile
A sacred vow impossible to resist –
And refuse to give up easily." – "But he must
Be stopped!" – "Yes, yes, my child – but how?" – "There's proof
Of what he did" – and showed him… He gaped. "The truth
Will out," was all he said.
                          Soon after, they
Attended the Welcome Party of her three-day

Wedding, with friends and family. Her rich father
Talked shop. There was much gossip, and much blather –

Until her oldest friends began to tell
Stories about her as a child – how well
She could climb trees – play football – read and write –
Tell *Märchen*, which were told her every night
By her mother's mother, a well-known *Märchenfrau*
Who'd scared her sometimes, reminding her of how
Mama had died in childbirth – she'd only known
A painting of her, dressed in her wedding gown…
"Tell us one now, my child," the priest suggested.
"Yes, tell us one, tell us one now!" they all requested.

"Why not?" she murmured: "A tale you've never heard –
A little gruesome, but please don't be scared.
'All's well that ends well', my grandmother said:
It was and is not so – and God forbid
Our lives should ever *be* a 'horror story'!"
Fox almost smiled to think how much more gory
Real life could be. No one told tales of *him*
As a boy. His father, and a sister, had not come
From Frankfurt. No one dared repeat a rumour,
Or crack a joke. He was not known for his humour…

Maria's '*Märchen*'

"*In Hanau, on the Kinzig, there once lived
A miller, born in Frankfurt, who had thrived
Away from home – become, in fact, so rich
That of all millers on the river, which
Had more than twenty mills, he took the cake…*
A *Märchen*'s just a *Märchen*, father. Take
My story how you will, no story's real."
– "And yet they *can* resemble – help reveal –
Whatever happened," the priest pontificated.
Maria's girlfriends giggled – whispered – waited…

"*One day the miller's daughter met by chance
At Hanau's yearly Harvest Festival dance
A certain Captain Wolf, who'd bought a house,
Left vacant in the deepest darkest Bulau's
Pathless interior – a place for fattening swine…*

The story isn't yours, my dear – or mine.
And anything may happen any time…
Whoever heard real people talk in rhyme?
– *The miller knew the family:* Rich, *he thought…*
The house was just the lair that Wolf had sought –

And though the rumour was he'd been a pirate,
With cash in hand he easily acquired it.
– A much-feared robber on the Spanish Main,
A captain who'd enjoyed inflicting pain –
Or worse – on culprits… The tales, of course, were many
And gory. Wolf had made a pretty penny:
The miller liked him. When he came to woo
The daughter, she was told to like him too.
This girl was neither timid, weak nor weepy.
But as for Captain Wolf, she found him creepy.

Her father remonstrated. And she had
Always obeyed him until now – felt bad
About not wanting to do something he
Insisted on so energetically;
So went to ask her favourite priest's advice.
The miller seldom prayed, but found it nice
That she *did… His family had been Huguenots –*
Like yours, dear father – who, as everyone knows,
Prefer their pie on the table… Before she died,
Her Catholic mother blessed her: Be brave, be good."

– "'Honour thy father and thy mother,'" said
The priest – "'in life, and after they are dead.'
– Excuse me, but that's what all priests would say.
And instruct her to confess her sins and pray…
Unless, that is, some just impediment
Arose – which might, then, rightfully prevent
Her doing what her father asked her to…"
– *"And so they were betrothed, although she knew*
Something was wrong. When Wolf turned up to greet her
He looked, she thought, as if he'd like to eat her…

One day he almost smiled: she'd not yet seen
The house in which she'd shortly be his queen:
'Let's have – why not? – a secret rendezvous.'
He licked his lips: 'Just me, the house, and you.'

– It may or may not come as a surprise,
Dearest, to hear that *your* unyielding eyes
Will not allow me either to say no...
– *Wolf eyed her: 'Next week's Easter. Will Wednesday do?*
I'll meet you at the footbridge by the river.'
Thinking of this next day, she started to quiver...

By Tuesday, though, she also thought Why not?
Perhaps she'd know then more exactly what
Her intuition told her was not right.
Or was she wrong about him? Awake in the night,
She was afraid of tales dismissed by day.
On Wednesday late wet snow fell, blocking the way
To the narrow bridge – on which he'd pinned a note
The night before, however, in his neat
But spiky hand... No one must see him show her
The primrose path to her pre-bridal bower...

Next day she was alone and – feeling bored –
Decided, since the snow had mostly thawed,
To find the house herself – she was sure she could,
And rode along the Kinzig into the wood...
April. The sun went in. But she could see
His note like a white bird nailed to a black tree.
– *'Be bold, ride on,' it said: 'turn right – left – right.*
The Wolf will see his fiancée home tonight!'"...
By now the groom had started sweating slightly;
Her father grinned – and tried to treat it lightly.

"It's just a story," the priest repeated: "You
Can't call it, therefore, either false or true"...
Some guests were bored; some found it rather provoking;
Maria's girlfriends thought she must be joking.
The old woman eavesdropped; other servants stared.
The priest said nothing more – watched Fox – prepared
For trouble. Maria watched her quarry as well,
Who in the meantime wished them all in hell –
But tried to suss how *much* Maria was wise to,
And guess what best to ignore, evade, or rise to...

"Across the wooden bridge," his bride went on,
"The track led into the forest. She had gone
Much further than she'd ever been before

When all at once a house with a green door
Appeared between the trees, and the path stopped.
The door swung on its hinges. Her heart hopped.
– An abandoned hunters' lodge? Perhaps. But how could
So broken-down a place, so deep in the wood,
Be Wolf's?... She stepped inside, and gasped – pale yellow
Firelight came flickering up the steps from the cellar.

She froze, afraid. But, then, crept slowly down.
A frail old woman was cooking. With a groan
She asked Maria why, of her own free will,
She'd come to that infernal place. She still
Had time to escape; but when Herr Wolf *returned...*
Beneath a blackened pot a red fire burned,
Boiling what looked like joints of salted pork:
She'd seen pigs' bones and ashes round the back.
– Suddenly, though, gruff curses! frantic screaming!...
Later, what followed seemed to her like dreaming

Nightmare on nightmare – which she couldn't shake
Her mind or body free of: wide awake,
She pinched her forearm purple making sure.
The old woman hid her. Lame, unwell and poor,
Unable to escape from Wolf on her own,
She'd always been the cook there – had stayed on,
After the hunters left... You know what's next,
Herr Fuchs." – "How *should* I know?" Fox snarled – pale, vexed,
And deeply shaken by Maria's nerve.
– "Hail, Mary!" whooped the priest, without reserve.

– "You raped the girl, and butchered her lovely limbs
As if they were a pig's." – "A hundred hymns
Of praise shall be recited to Maria!" –
"You salted, boiled, and washed her down with beer.
The pile of bones and ashes, the old woman told me,
Were not a pig's... Dear father, please don't scold me,
I cannot marry this man-monster." – "I
Emphatically, categorically deny
Her every allegation." – "Your drunken snorting
And sated grunts accompanied our parting.

Your cook can testify to all I say." –
"A lying hag! A witch! And, anyway,
Where is she now?" – "Behind you. Small and light,
She lay in my blood-soaked lap that snowy night,
And both of us rode home." – "*Your* blood-soaked lap!
Soaked with whose blood?" – "To steal her rings you chopped
The poor girl's fingers off. One flew through the air
And landed behind the hunters' hogshead, where
I sat in terror on the dirty floor":
She pulled it from her apron – "Need I say more?"

The game was up. Fox made a run for it;
Her father blocked the doorway. In a fit
Of furious energy, the pirate lunged
About him with his captain's sword, and plunged
It deep in the corpulent belly of one guest –
Then in his wife's décolleté left breast.
The miller, in the fray, was seen to stagger –
And died that evening, stabbed by Fox's dagger…
The priest, defrocked for blasphemous behaviour,
Married Maria – each other's loving saviour.

7   THE TWO SONS

> *"And he said, A certain man had two sons:*
> *And the younger of them said, Father, give unto me the portion of goods that falleth to me.*
> *And he divided unto them his living.*
> *And the younger son gathered all together, and took his journey into a far country, and there wasted his substance with riotous living…*
> *And when he had spent all, there arose a mighty famine in that land; and he began to be in want.*
> *And he went and joined himself to a citizen of that country; and he sent him into his fields to feed swine.*
> *And he would fain have filled his belly with the husks that the swine did eat: and no man gave unto him."*
> – Luke XV.11–16

i   The Father to His Younger Son

Dear Son,
           They say you're going abroad
Again, so let me here record
More than I think I've ever said
About what happened. When I'm dead
You'll want to know: sons always do.
Remember, I had a father, too.
His face was impassive. A silent mask.
Now it's too late for me to ask.

When you left, a fit of fury smashed
The last of my patience. The cheques you'd cashed! –
The bonds, the land – by rights, mine still –
All sold, all gone – against my will.
But I'd make you suffer, I'd make you pay!
What would friends – colleagues – neighbours – say?
I felt like a fool. My son was a rake.
I'd given. But all you'd done was take!

My self-respect was badly dented.
For months I raged. I deeply resented
The sight of your picture, the sound of your name.
When I heard you were broke, resentment and shame
Gave way to virulent *Schadenfreude:*

"Now you can work," I thought, "you avoider
Of all things strenuous, hard or risky:
Pigs can be very mean and frisky!"

You'll remember the only letter I sent,
Announcing my father's death, which meant
More than I'd ever have thought it could
To me. My own flesh, my own blood,
Seemed closer now with every breath
To the pain and horror of such a death.
They'd amputated. The wound and his pride
Rankled and festered until he died.

In one so old, such agony
Pierced all my defences. Not that he
Had shown compassion. A righteous man,
He accused as only a father can.
But now he was dead. So what had he got
From fearing his neighbours' *Thou-shalt-not?*
From judging his children, despising his wife?
By the time he died he hated life.

Which helped me to understand a thing
Or two. If, in anger and fear, we cling
To what's here today but gone tomorrow,
Our joys begin and end in sorrow,
Our loves in hatred. And so what frees
The imprisoned soul must be to release
What no one can keep in any case.
In the end the least we lose is face...

Until it was finally clear to me
I had to let you go – let you be.
When I saw you, I *felt* my blood revive:
The lost had been found, the dead was alive!
Revenge is a *self*-destructive duty:
Forgiveness a flower of rooted Beauty.
Nature forgets. Live here today –
And eat, drink, love, laugh, weep, sing, pray

Glad prayers of praise – and praise again –
And thanks for life, death, joy and pain!
Nothing endures. And nor will you.

So what? Let what you choose to do
Accord with how you freely *are*
In your heart and mind. And may you share
This goal with others – to let life be.
Goodbye, my son. Come home to me.

ii   The Elder Brother

At last he's gone. And bloody good riddance!
He only came back because he was hungry.
The business has never been the same
Since he sold his share to total strangers,
And grandfather snuffed it. The tangible dangers –
The buy-outs I've countered! And I'm *not to blame.*
Is it any wonder it makes me angry?
I'd have him working here for a pittance!

Instead of which I expect he's completed
Some backstairs deal or special arrangement
With father. He always gets it right
When it comes to pampering number one.
And now I suppose it's beach and sun
While I slave at the office day and night
Without so much as a thank-you for payment.
Is it any wonder I feel cheated?

But if he *had much say we'd all go under.*
So perhaps it's as well that he's done a bunk.
Though the first time he dropped us, father and I
Also fell out. I was busting a gut
To keep the business going. But
A favourite's a favourite. And that's why –
Though his best ideas are nothing but junk –
He's always managed to steal my thunder.

I refused to join their song and dance.
What madness to throw a welcome-home party
For a son who's wasted what was yours!
As a thank-you for making your life-time shorter?
Who I wouldn't trust with my wife or daughter,
Though they say he prefers expensive whores.

Yet women all like these arty-farty
Idlers with endless time on their hands.

And they've always liked him. *But he'll never marry:*
Too frivolous, too work-shy. He'll never settle
In any one place with a proper job.
And as for children, they'd soon show him
Action talks louder than words – song – poem,
Money than any gift of the gab…
Nothing, though, puts him on his mettle –
And cans are for other people to carry.

But if he imagines father's forgotten
What happened, he's very much mistaken.
No one forgives such flippant folly
For ever. At some point he'll get his come-uppance.
He's self-destructive. I wouldn't give tuppence
For his future. After he'd wasted the lolly,
It was grandfather's death that saved his bacon:
Our loss was his gain. But the gain was ill-gotten.

Father was shattered, and in need of distraction.
If he still hasn't finally come to his senses,
I'll poison the wells while Junior's away.
I'd love to know just what he's up to:
He's too conniving – too corrupt – to
Be off on an innocent holiday.
Just getting behind his strategic defences
Would give me more than satisfaction.

He'd like to be one of the idle rich:
I'll show him his castles are built in the air.
He thinks that money grows on trees:
I'll work on father. It's gone too far.
They say he was born under a lucky star –
But we'll see about that. And we'll see who sees
The way things are. By Christ, I swear
I'll do what I can to queer his pitch.

iii The Younger Son to His Father

Dear Father,
              What I hated most
Was how *little* you had to say to me.
But my brother controlled the company.
In the end I gave you up for lost,
And left. I didn't mean to hurt
You badly. But the rows we'd had! –
And the times you'd treated Mother like dirt,
Till she left as well. Big brother, big dad,

How I despised your money-grubbing!
But I was above all that. Or below it.
What else should I do with your money but blow it?
Shop-lifting was fun, too – rightfully robbing
The stinking rich. Free love was in,
And all your family values out.
There was really no such thing as sin:
Sex, drugs, the arts – we had no doubt

That we were right. I had real friends
At last – without self-interest
Or envy. But, later, the best
Gloated the most. Thus friendship ends
In thicker shit than where it started,
And nobody helped a human pig
Among the pigs that grubbed – fucked – farted
Contentedly. Dreading what you and my prig

Of a brother would do or say, I shat
My pride and my guts out in unhygienic,
Primitive, half-starved, damp, if scenic
Conditions. Your letter changed all that.
Was the old man dead? – And what if *you* died? –
Or I? That morning, not so far from it,
With a stolen flagon of *vino* I'd
Woken half-choked on vomit.

Which might have killed you too. So I,
By suffering, caused suffering. My heartless fears
And guilts were gradually softened by tears
Of empathy. Now a worm or fly

Shares my inalienable right to live,
For life is ordinary *and* divine,
And the human power to remember / forgive
Is beyond both pigs and bottom line.

So why – and how far – am I going? Or not?
Elsewhere's a place / thought / word on the way
To – nowhere. Once the mind is free
From obsession, struggling madly to get
Rich quick – to the top – on – in on – away;
Once then is now, and there is here,
And days and nights become one day,
Joy dispels anger, love dispels fear.

In our *hearts* we know that this is true.
But still we must redream ourselves
Till the clenched block of the will dissolves,
And leaves us freer to be and do.
When abroad, I exist at one remove
From the force of such clinging forms of sorrow
As too much home – and too much love
That's here today but gone tomorrow.

To withdraw is not to advance. From elsewhere
I hope to watch and listen better –
Less blind to routine roles – to the fear
Of forces and forms which cease to matter
As place recedes. And I hope to return
To enough, not too much. To be free is to grow:
As time recedes, I hope to learn
To let life be by letting it go.

An East / West Epilogue

For the word of God is quick, and powerful, and sharper than any two-edged sword, piercing even to the dividing asunder of soul and spirit, and of the joints and marrow, and is a discerner of the thoughts and intents of the heart.
Hebrews IV.12

The word of the Lord is right;... He loveth righteousness and judgement... By the word of the Lord were the heavens made; and all the host of them by the breath of his mouth.
Psalm XXXIII.4–6

Words are not just wind. Words have something to say. But if what they have to say is not fixed, then do they really say something? Or do they say nothing?... Suppose you and I have had an argument. If you have beaten me instead of my beating you, then are you necessarily right and am I necessarily wrong? If I have beaten you instead of your beating me, then am I necessarily right and are you necessarily wrong? If you and I don't know the answer, then other people are bound to be even more in the dark.
Chuang Tzu, ch.2

1   AESOPEAN (3)

"Give not that which is holy unto the dogs, neither cast ye your pearls before swine, lest they trample them under their feet, and turn again and rend you."
– *Matthew VII.6*

"And the lion showed to Jerome his foot, being hurt… Then this holy man put thereto diligent cure, and healed him, and he abode ever after as a tame beast with [him]."
– *The Golden Legend (ca.* 1265)

i

As if two travellers crossed a land
Inhabited only by monkeys:
The King, his family, courtiers, and
Their relatives, slaves, and flunkeys.

As if one traveller was a liar
And flattered the King *et al*
When asked, at a banquet, to compare
Their race with other people.

As if the second told the truth,
Because he thought we should –
And cut the crap. The aftermath
Was buckets of truthful blood.

The first could then decide: to lie
And stay – perhaps do well;
Or, elsewhere, choose more freely why –
How – *what* to tell / not tell.

ii

Knocked to the ground, a bat was once
Caught by a weasel, who
Detested mice. The bat was no dunce:
She trilled *I'm a bird!* And flew.

Another dusk, another weasel –
Who hated birds: *I'm a mouse!...*

'WHO *AM* I?' – Resolving the ancient puzzle
Takes nerve as well as nous.

iii

Under a lion's big paw, a rat
Shrieked, *Let me go, my Lord!*
I'm not a useless mouse or bat. –
And, soon, she'd bravely gnawed
Him free of a snare of ropes and gut...
The King, though, wasn't just angry
(With trappers / life / wife / subjects...), but –
This time – felt rather hungry.

iv

A dog-fox and old roué of a goat
With his loud-mouthed friend, a cock,
Met one hot noon. The goat's hoarse throat
Was dry with boasting. The fox

Jumped first into a well he knew.
But then?... *I'll climb on your horns –*
Fetch help. The help*less* doodle-doo
Welcomed no more cold dawns.

v

A peasant took a big black sheep
To market. Jill nagged him, "Jack,
Bring cash. And if you touch a drop,
Just wait till you come back!"

Six poor but humorous neighbours hoaxed
Their tipsy friend. One after
Another, they greeted and tried to coax
Him (stifling snorts of laughter)

To sell his big black *dog*. "It's not
A dog, it's a sheep," Jack said.
But by the third or fourth was a lot
Less sure. His addled head

Decided he'd best go home soon. Strife
Erupted when Jack confessed
To his infuriated wife
That he'd also thought it best

To give so strange a beast away.
Six neighbours couldn't be wrong –

Who sheared, butchered, and sold it next day,
Not *for* but *with* a song.

vi

A hunter killed a furious lion.
His donkey stole its skin,
And slouched about the fields, defying
Hunters and all their kin.

His appearance frightened friend and foe.
A fox, though, heard him bray:
He roared *Hee-haw, hee-haw* – and so
Gave his dumb self away.

His master failed to find this funny,
And in the ensuing fracas
The much-feared donkey died… But honey
Was shortly found in his carcass.

vii

A poor old woodman, bearing a bundle
Of firewood which bowed his back,
Collapsed, half-hoping to rekindle
His strength, by the icy track.

His muscles were quivering, then grew stiff.
A blizzard began to blow.
His feet and fingers froze, as if
Already buried by snow.

Life was too hard. He wished he was dead.
Death came. Then life seemed good!
When the Horror beckoned, he begged him instead
To help him carry the wood.

viii

Some hens had found a water-jar
Left out in the heat and dust:
Unable to stick their heads in far
Enough, *It's empty*, they fussed.

A raven dropped some stones in the water,
Till it rose and he could drink:
Bird-brains are bird-brains, he kraaked – *they ought to
LOOK before they think!*

ix

A rooting rooster dug up a pearl:
You must be worth a lot!
How pretty you'd look, he clucked, *on a girl.*
But I need things to eat.

*

A son was left a library
Of books, and noticed this one:
"Poems," he grunted. "No use to me:
I cannot spend – eat – kiss one!"

Smiling, he auctioned all he could
And threw the rest away,
Which were his father's ghostly food
And drink from day to day.

        *

Satan said, *Turn these stones into bread!*
Jesus, "By bread alone
We die. – Whereas my words," he added,
"Outlast all pearls / all swine."

x

Can small be big? A tiny ant
Fell in a river. A dove
Dropped her a leaf…
                – *If you should want*
My *help one day…* Above

Them both she glimpsed two greedy eyes
Trained on her pure white friend –
And bit. The hunter, caught by surprise,
Shot wide. Thus lives depend.

xi

A pregnant bitch – shut out in the bitter
Cold of mid-winter – creeping –
In search of a lair to bear her litter –
Almost as if she were weeping –

Passed a soft-hearted sheep-dog, who
Invited her in: *I'll sleep*

Elsewhere, my dear, for a night or two.
There now. You needn't weep.

But she wept again next day: six pups
Would *die* outside in the cold!!...
The sheep-dog knew about life's ups
And downs, and slept by the fold.

All summer she slept in the open air
Beneath the fresh green trees.
In autumn, feeling she'd done her share,
She asked for her den back, please.

Alas, six snarling brutes and their beast
Of a mother stood their ground:
Well, well, my puppies, she thought. *At least*
You grew up safe and sound.

xii

Jerome was studying in his cave.
The desert night was cold.
A lion roared and roared. Though brave,
The saint was weak and old.

But pulled the thorn, and dressed the wound.
The lion stayed. At ease,
Jerome wrote on. No sight or sound
Disturbed his inner peace.

2   NATHAN THE WISE – A MEDLEY

"Sind Christ und Jude eher Christ und Jude,
Als Mensch?" – Lessing

> When Saladin captured Jerusalem,
> Resurrecting the eternal question
> Of who should rule the Holy Land –
> Moslem (or Jew) or Christian? –
>
> Though the kings and queens of Jerusalem
> Had neglected their Christian duty,
> And long indulged in vice and intrigue
> And a predilection for booty,
>
> Richard I and Philip of France
> And a band of zealous Crusaders
> Set sail to wreak their righteous wrath
> On the Saracen invaders.
>
> And *Kaiser Rotbart* led a host
> Of the Good against this Badness:
> Alas, he drowned while bathing in
> The River Calycadnus!
>
> Since when he waits with his band of knights,
> In a mountain called Kyffhäuser –
> *"Man baute nicht Rom an einem Tag"* –
> To return as Germany's Kaiser…
>
> But the royal fleets hove to – where a siege
> Was already in furious session –
> At Acre, which the Moslems held:
> Nine tenths of the game is possession.
>
> The soldiers of Christ and the Prophet fought;
> An uneasy truce resulted.
> The French and English squabbled and bitched.
> The Jews were not consulted,

So Nathan went on a business trip
To Babylon, where he made an
Outstanding profit, both in cash
And camels, fully laden.

With soldiers of fortune everywhere,
Out to pillage and forage,
This journey of several hundred miles
Took cunning as well as courage.

Back home in Jerusalem, a fire
Had almost killed his daughter:
A Templar had risked his life for hers,
Malgré the general slaughter.

Recha was eighteen years of age.
Which father would not have exchanged all
He had to save her life? She thought
Her rescuer was an angel.

The proud young Templar's life had been spared
By Saladin, no other,
Because, as the Sultan raised his sword,
He saw his younger brother,

Assad, who twenty years before
Had inexplicably vanished.
Saladin's scimitar sank to the ground
And the Templar fled, astonished.

When Nathan tried to thank him, he
Declared he'd have no dealings
With well-off Jews – even if he hurt
A young Jewess's feelings.

Nathan's wise words soon change his mind –
And so does Recha's beauty.
They fall in love. He searches his soul:
What now is his Christian duty?

Meanwhile the Sultan too has heard
Of Nathan. Short of money,
He sends for this rich inhabitant
Of the land of milk and honey.

The scene is an audience chamber in
His palace. Servants scurry.
He complains to his sister, Sittah, that
The Jew is in no hurry.

To calm him, Sittah says, "Perhaps
They simply couldn't find him."
Saladin: Ah, sister, sister!
Sittah: You behave
As though a frightful battle
Were starting.
Saladin: Yes, with weapons which
I've never learned to handle:
Thrusting and parrying with nothing but words –
Defending my position –
Leading him on to slippery ground.
When have I ever practised
Such tactics? And for what? To fish
For money. To frighten
Money out of a Jew. Money! Am I
Reduced to petty tricks to gain
A trifle?
Sittah: Every trifle,
Brother, too lightly spurned,
Takes its revenge.
Saladin: True. All too true.
But what if now this Jew
Is the good and sensible man
They say he is?
Sittah: Then there's no further
Problem. The snare is set
Only for miserly, anxious,
Timorous Jews: not for the good
And wise. That sort is ours
Already, without a snare. The pleasure
Of hearing him excuse himself –
With what Samsonian strength
He snaps the cord, or with what sly

| | Solicitude he wriggles past
| | Your nets – that further pleasure
| | Is yours as well.
Saladin: True. I look forward
| | To it.
Sittah: What other problem can
| | Embarrass you? Since if he's one
| | Of the usual crowd, he's nothing but
| | A Jew like any Jew – and, surely,
| | You needn't be ashamed to appear
| | As he imagines all men are? What's more,
| | Whoever tries to play a better role
| | Will seem in his eyes a fool, a clown.
Saladin: You mean
| | I'd better now *act* badly
| | So that the bad will not think badly
| | Of my good behaviour?
Sittah: Yes, if 'badly'
| | Means acting in accordance
| | With how things are.
Saladin: And what
| | Could any woman's mind devise
| | That a Jew could not gloze over?
Sittah: Gloze over!
Saladin: I fear such barbed and delicate things
| | Would break in my awkward hands. Such wiles
| | Must be performed as devised – with sharpness,
| | With nimbleness. In any case,
| | I'll dance the way I can. And rather worse
| | Than better.
Sittah: Now, brother, don't be bashful.
| | I'd take your place, if only you'd let me.
| | Men of your sort would have us women believe
| | That their sword and nothing but their sword
| | Has got them where they are. The lion
| | Is ashamed to hunt with the fox – but ashamed
| | Of foxes, not of cunning.
Saladin: And how
| | You women like to get us men
| | Down to your level! Now go. I think
| | I've conned my lesson.
Sittah: What? Am I to go?
Saladin: You wish to stay?

Sittah: Well, if not stay,
At least to be in earshot – here
In the next room.
Saladin: There? To eavesdrop? No, sister,
I insist. I hear the curtains – he's coming.
Away with you! Don't linger in there. I'll look.

(Exit Sittah. Saladin seats himself as Nathan enters)

Saladin: Come closer, Jew, come closer. Closer still.
Have no fear.
Nathan: May your enemies fear you.
Saladin: Your name is Nathan?
Nathan: Yes.
Saladin: Nathan the Wise?
Nathan: No.
Saladin: No, indeed. And yet they call you "wise".
Nathan: Perhaps. The people.
Saladin: Do not imagine
I treat what the people say with contempt.
For a long time I've wanted to meet the man
They call "the Wise".
Nathan: And what if they
Call him "the Wise" from spite? Or "wise"
Means only clever? And "clever" means
He knows what's good for him – and how
To get it?
Saladin: Truly good, you mean?
Nathan: Then, clearly, the man with most self-interest
Is cleverest. And, clearly, clever and wise
Are one.
Saladin: A position – equally clearly – which
You mean to abandon. What's truly best
The people hardly know. But you
Know it. Or seek to know it. Or
Have thought about it. That alone
Makes a man wise.
Nathan: Which each presumes
Himself to be.
Saladin: Enough of this modesty.
Nothing but modesty where one expects
Plain common sense is nauseous. Let's
Get down to business. But

              Be honest, Jew. Be honest.
Nathan: Sultan,
              I hope to serve you now so well
              As to ensure your future custom.
Saladin: Serve me? How?
Nathan: The best of all
              Is yours – and at the cheapest
              Prices.
Saladin: The best? Of what? Not, surely,
              Your goods? My sister, Jew, will haggle
              Over your prices. I am not
              A merchant among merchants.
Nathan: Then
              Doubtless you'd like to know if I
              Noticed – or even met – the enemy,
              Who's on the move again, they say,
              While travelling? – When out in the open, I…
Saladin: That's also not the reason
              I asked you here. I know enough
              About all that. In short, …
Nathan: Sultan?
Saladin: I'd like to hear your teaching on
              Other, quite different questions. Since
              You possess such wisdom, tell me
              Which of the faiths, which of the laws,
              Has brought you most enlightenment?
Nathan: Sultan,
              I am a Jew.
Saladin: And I a Moslem.
              The Christian comes between us. Three
              Religions. But only one of them
              True. A man like yourself will hardly
              Stay where the accident of birth
              Threw him. Or, if he does, he stays
              For reasons, choosing what's better
              With insight. Well now, tell me which reasons –
              Which insights – you have, of the sort which I
              Have lacked the time to meditate
              Upon. Tell me which choice you've made,
              Determined by these reasons, so
              That I – in confidence, of course –
              Might make it mine. You hesitate?
              You weigh me with your eyes. It may

     Well be that I'm the first, as Sultan,
     To have such idle notions – which
     Seem not entirely unworthy, though,
     Of a sultan, don't you think? Then speak,
     Tell me! Or would you like a moment
     To set your thoughts in order? Good! I grant it.
     Think then, think quickly. In a moment
     I'll return.

(He goes into the next room, after Sittah.)

Nathan: Strange, strange. Now what am I
     To make of this? What does the Sultan
     Want? I anticipated money. But
     Truth? And truth in cash – a blank cheque – as if
     The truth were coins! Well, ancient coins
     Perhaps, weighed in the balance. Only
     Our modern coins, made valid
     By nothing but a stamp, for counting
     On counters, tell no truth. Are men
     To pocket truth in their minds
     Like cash in sacks? Now who's more Jew,
     I or he? But wait. What if the Sultan
     In truth is not demanding truth? And yet
     The chance that he might make a trap
     Of truth is small – too small.
     Too small? For one as great as he
     Nothing's too small. Yes, yes. He blurted
     It out too quickly. One chooses one's words,
     One listens, when approaching another in friendship.
     I must take care. But how? To be
     Utterly Jew won't help. And to be
     No Jew at all still less. Because
     If not a Jew, he might well ask,
     Why not a Moslem? Wait! Now that
     Might save me. Stories are food for more
     Than children. Here he comes. Well, let him.

(Saladin returns)

Saladin: Am I too hasty? Have you gathered
     Your thoughts? Then speak. Nobody's here
     To hear us.

Nathan: May the world
Hear us!
Saladin: Is Nathan then so sure
In such a matter? Ha! That's what I call
Wisdom! Never to conceal
The truth! To wager all
One has: life and limb, goods and blood!
Nathan: When need be, yes. And if
It helps.
Saladin: From today may I deserve
My title of *Reformer of*
The World and of the Law!
Nathan: A fine
Title. But, Sultan, before confiding
In you entirely, may I tell you
A little story?
Saladin: Why not? I've always
Been fond of little stories, well
Told.
Nathan: Alas, I've little talent
For telling them well.
Saladin: Again so proudly
Modest! But continue.
Nathan: Long ago
There lived in the East a man
Who had a priceless ring
From one who loved him. The stone, an opal, had
A hundred lovely colours, and
Possessed the secret power
To make whoever wore it – provided
He wore it in good faith –
Beloved of God and man.
No wonder, therefore, that this man
Wore it at all times, and took pains
To keep it in his family
For ever. How? He left it to
His favourite son, and stipulated
That he in turn should leave it to
His favourite son – which favourite son,
Without regard to birthright, was to be
Head of the house through the ring's power
Alone.
Saladin: I understand. Go on.

Nathan: And so the ring was passed from son to son
Until it reached the father of three sons
All three of whom were equally obedient,
All three of whom he loved
Equally. Or rather, at different times,
First the one, then the other, and now
The third – while each alone
Was with him, while his loving heart
Was undivided by the other two –
Seemed worthiest of the ring, which he
In innocent weakness promised
To each. Until his death
Approached, and the good old man
Wondered what he should do. It pained him
To have to disappoint at least
Two of his trusting sons. At last
He sent in secret for a skilful craftsman
From whom he ordered two
New rings, identical in appearance
To the first, and neither cost
Nor trouble would he spare
Until the rings were matched. The craftsman
Matched them. So that the father, when he saw
All three, was quite unable
To distinguish one from another. Relieved
And happy, one at a time he called
His sons and one at a time
Gave each a ring – and blessed him – and
Died. Do you hear me, Sultan?
Saladin: I hear,
I hear. But end your story soon.
Nathan: I'm at the end. What happens next
Is obvious. Their father dead, the sons
Arrive, each with his ring, and each
Claiming to be the head
Of the house. They check, they quarrel,
They wail. In vain. No one could prove
Which ring was true.

(He pauses, expecting the Sultan to reply.)

                    Almost as little
As anyone now can prove

	Which of the faiths, which of the laws,
	Is true.
Saladin:	What? Is that your answer
	To my question?
Nathan:	A mere excuse
	For not trusting myself to try
	To tell those rings apart
	Which the father intended no one
	Should tell apart.
Saladin:	The rings, the rings! Don't trifle
	With me! Surely, three such
	Religions can be told apart
	With ease! Down to their clothing, food
	And drink.
Nathan:	But not their grounds, because
	Their grounds all lie in history, do they not? –
	Written or handed down. And history
	Is taken in good faith – on trust.
	Well then, whose faith and trust
	Does one doubt least? One's own,
	One's forebears': the faith of those whose love
	Has proved itself to us from childhood on,
	Who never let us down – unless
	To do us good. How can I trust
	My forebears less than you trust yours?
	Or vice versa. How can I
	Demand of you that you belie
	Your forebears so as not to differ
	From mine? Or vice versa. And
	The same applies to Christians, am I right?

(The Sultan says nothing.)

        But let's continue our story. The sons
        Eventually brought their case before
        A judge. And each son swore
        He'd had the ring directly from
        His father – which was true –
        Having been promised many times by him
        That one day he'd enjoy the rights
        The ring bestowed. The father,
        Each son averred, could not have wanted
        To trick him. Rather than suspect

	So dear a parent, he
	Could not but blame his brothers, who
	He otherwise was happy to believe
	Were excellent fellows. But
	He'd be revenged on them as traitors
	By bringing both to justice.
Saladin:	And
	The judge? What would you have the judge
	Say? Speak!
Nathan:	The judge said, "Bring your father
	Before me here – or I'll dismiss
	The case! Am I to sit in judgement
	On riddles? Or shall the true
	Ring open its mouth and speak?
	But wait! I hear the ring possesses
	A magic power – to make one loved,
	Beloved of God and man. Now that
	Decides it! Clearly, the false rings won't
	Possess such power. So which of you
	Is loved the most by the other two?
	Speak up! What? Silence? Ah, the rings
	Only work inwards, not
	Outwards! Each loves himself
	The most. Then all of you must be
	Deceived deceivers! All three rings
	Are false. The one true ring
	Must have got lost. To hide
	Or to replace the loss, your father
	Had three rings made for the one."
Saladin:	Brilliant!
Nathan:	"And so," the judge went on, "if you
	Want my advice instead of my verdict: Take
	Things as they are. Each one of you
	Has now received a ring from his father:
	So let each one believe his ring
	The true one. Perhaps your father
	No longer wanted a single ring
	To tyrannize his house. It's clear
	He loved you all, and loved you
	Equally: two were not to suffer
	For the sake of one. Well then, let each
	Imitate such impartial,
	Such incorruptible love! compete

                To make the power of the stone in his ring
                As clear as daylight; assist
                This power with loving kindness, heart-felt
                Peacefulness, good deeds, deep
                Submission to the will of God. And when
                In more than a thousand thousand years
                The powers of these stones are clearly manifest
                Among your children's children's children,
                Then I invite them to come in their turn
                Before this court. A wiser judge
                Than I will sit here then. Now go!" So said
                The modest judge.

Saladin: God! God!
Nathan: Saladin,
                In case you should feel that you
                Are this promised wiser man…
Saladin (rushing up to him and grasping his hand, which he continues to hold):
                                          I? am dust. I
                Am nothing. O God!
Nathan: What is it, Sultan?
Saladin: Nathan,
                The thousand thousand years of your judge
                Are not yet over. His seat of judgement is
                Not mine. Go. Go! But be my friend.
Nathan: Has Saladin nothing further
                To ask me?
Saladin: Nothing.
Nathan: Nothing?
Saladin: Nothing. Why?
Nathan: I would have welcomed the opportunity
                To ask a favour.
Saladin: Favours need
                No opportunity. Speak.
Nathan: Having returned
                Only today from a long journey
                On business, I almost have too much
                Money. And times are looking
                Dangerous again. Unsure
                Of where to keep it safe, I thought
                That you perhaps – since impending war
                Always demands more money – might
                Require some.
Saladin (looking him in the eye):

	Nathan, I won't ask
	With whom you've spoken. Nor
	What caution – what suspicion –
	Might otherwise have prompted
	This offer…
Nathan:	Suspicion?
Saladin:	Which
	I deserve. Forgive me! What's the point?
	I admit it. Yes, I was, as it happens,
	Wondering –
Nathan:	Not whether to ask
	For such a loan?
Saladin:	Precisely.
Nathan:	Why then,
	That suits us both – although I can't yet send
	You all my cash, since first
	I mean to pay a handsome sum
	To the young Templar, whom
	You know, of course.
Saladin:	A Templar? Surely
	You won't support my bitterest foe
	As well?
Nathan:	I mean the Templar
	Whose life you spared.
Saladin:	Ah, yes! Now I'd
	Forgotten all about him! And you
	Know him? Where is he?
Nathan:	What?
	Have you not heard how much of your mercy
	Has flowed through him to me? Risking
	His freshly granted life, he rescued
	My daughter from death by fire.
Saladin:	Did he
	Indeed! Ha! That's how he looked!
	My brother, whom he resembles, would
	Have done the same! Is he still here?
	Bring him to me! I have told my sister
	So much about her brother, whom
	She never knew, that she
	Must see his double. Go
	And fetch him. Out of one good deed,
	Though born of nothing but passion,
	So much may grow! But go and fetch

This fire-defying Templar.
Business can wait.

(Exit Nathan)

Saladin: Well, now I wish
I'd let my sister listen.
How will I ever tell her this?
The rings! Long may they flourish! –

Also as intermarriage rings –
Simply from Man to Woman.
For surely Moslem, Christian and Jew
Have so much more in common

As human creatures now than their ways
Of doing things still differ.
My Assad would have been a man
For Richard the Lion-heart's sister!

And Sittah, were this truce a peace,
Might marry Richard's brother…

*

But soon both sides were busy again
Massacring one another.

The siege of Acre having resumed,
The Sultan replenished its garrisons.
One hundred thousand Christians died,
And God knows how many Saracens…

But not before strange things emerged
In the comedy's happy ending,
For Nathan had an enlightened heart
Which was truly worth befriending.

Returning from another trip
Once upon a time he'd found
His entire family dead and his house
Razed to the smoking ground.

He'd howled and wept and raged and cursed
His fate and God, who smashes
Our hopes to bits. He'd lain three days
And nights in sack-cloth and ashes,

Swearing implacable hatred towards
The Christians, who had murdered
Every Jew – man, woman and child –
In Gath, until he thought he'd

Never get up again. When he did,
He found a Christian brother
Who bore in his arms a little child
Which had lost its German mother

And oriental father, whose
Last wish had been to send
His daughter to the Jew who was
His most reliable friend.

Receiving the baby, Nathan knelt
And thanked inscrutable Heaven
For already giving him one back
In return for taking seven.

This child was Recha. Before they'd returned
From her German birthplace, her parents
Had also had a son, whom they left
With his uncle, whose forbearance

Nurtured the proud young Templar who
Eventually rescued his sister
From death by fire. It was a bit
Of luck he hadn't kissed her.

But, even stranger, their father was found
To be Saladin's missing brother. –
And none of this was known before
They'd fallen in love with each other…

The Templar blenched and Recha blushed.
But soon they were looking jauntier:
Saladin was their uncle now,
And Sittah was their aunty. –

A happy melting pot! And yet
Give me the doubting Thomases,
With their hands in the sacred vision's wound:
Art is too full of promises

No life can honour – any more
Than, after the end of the drama,
When Acre fell, the Christians behaved
Like knights in shining armour.

Richard was king of the castle. And so,
To show how he meant to boss it, he
Lost his temper one hot afternoon
And committed a gross atrocity.

To speed up negotiations, three
Thousand men's heads were hacked off.
Saladin watched from a nearby hill.
Even his crack troops backed off.

Some Christian prisoners were therefore taught
What happens if you insult an
All-powerful, world- and law-reforming
Macho Egyptian sultan.

Terror was useful in a war
Chaotic and scarcely plannable;
The infidel horde was even convinced
Coeur de Lion was a cannibal.

Not only did he miss his pork,
They whispered, but certain ambassadors
Were served with boiled and bloated heads.
Now this was worse than hazardous –

And put the Moslems off their food.
Not that we need to credit it:
The rumour alone unmanned the Crescent,
Whoever may have fed it it.

But the Sultan prayed and fasted and lopped
Any who disobeyed orders.
He had a very strong right arm,
And a bodyguard of sworders.

And so the war raged back and forth
Till both of the armies were sick of it.
Saladin's health began to fail,
And though Richard was still in the thick of it

The perfidious Philip had made his adieus
And was bearding the Lion by invading
The defenceless duchy of Normandy –
Which was what you got for crusading.

Three hundred thousand Christians had died
And God knows how many Saracens,
Before these heroes finally tired
Of slaughtering each other's garrisons.

A three-year truce was agreed. The king
Of England departed quickly.
Saladin died at Damascus. His health
Had declined to very sickly.

The display of a shroud, not a standard, pronounced
Life wanes, death always waxes.
"The noblest monument of his fame"
(Gibbon) – the Saladine taxes –

Turned out too lucrative by far
To expire with their occasion,
And all the church's tithes and tenths
Accrued from this foundation.

"This pecuniary emolument
Certainly must have tended
To increase the interest of the popes
In Palestine." Thus ended

The Third Crusade. The Seventh and last
Took place a hundred years later.
The Christians lost. Their remnants retired
Into the fortress of Acre,

Where vice and business boomed for a time.
When their plundering became a nuisance
Khalil, the sultan, welcomed the chance
To demonstrate his puissance:

"After a siege of thirty-three days
The double wall was captured
By the Moslems, and the tallest tower
Surrendered to their engines;

"The Mamalukes made a general assault;
The city was stormed, and death or

slavery was the lot of sixty thousand Christians. The convent, or rather fortress, of the Templars resisted three days longer; but the great master was pierced with an arrow, and, of five hundred knights only ten were left alive, less happy than the victims of the sword, if they lived to suffer on a scaffold in the unjust and cruel proscription of the whole order. The king of Jerusalem, the patriarch, and the great master of the hospital effected their retreat to the shore; but the sea was rough, the vessels were insufficient, and great numbers of the fugitives were drowned before they could reach the isle of Cyprus... By the command of the sultan the churches and fortifications of the Latin cities were demolished: a motive of avarice or fear still opened the holy sepulchre to some devout and defenceless pilgrims: and a mournful and solitary silence prevailed along the coast which had so long resounded with the WORLD'S DEBATE."

(1996 / 2001)

3   AESOPEAN (4) – AFTER CHUANG TZU

"Men of the world suppose that form and colour, name and sound are sufficient to convey the truth of a thing. Because in the end they are not sufficient to convey truth, 'those who know do not speak, those who speak do not know'. But how can the world understand this?"
– Chuang Tzu, ch.13

i

The Duke of Ch'i sat quietly reading
The fables of Chuang Tzu.
His wheelwright asked him why – "Succeeding
Is something which we *do* –

Cannot be learned from books," he declared…
The wheelwright was clearly proud
Of his skills. The learned Duke concurred
In part – and read aloud:

"What use are words? One butcher's knife
Stays sharp because he cuts.
Another's is notched: he lives his life
By hacking. Ifs and buts

Can neither explain nor teach the art
Of cutting. Description confuses
Mere words with things they fail to impart.

And yet – words have their uses."

ii

A logic chopper mocked Chuang Tzu:
"A big and useless tree –
A gnarled ailanthus stump-sprout – too
Twisted for carpentry –

Has grown in my garden. Big vague words,
Likewise, are good for nothing."
Chuang Tzu smiled back: "All kinds of birds
Can rest with pleasure, or sing

In the shade of so high and broad a tree.
Men rest beneath it — even
Choppers of logic. Which is why
They call it 'tree-of-heaven'.

No one will cut it down for its wood.
Why should it come to grief?
It's neither bad nor very good.
Nothing will shorten its life."

iii

From his superior point of view
An oak condoled with a reed:

My dear, why don't you try to grow
Closer to me? My shade

Would help you to withstand the sun,
My strength the wildest storm…

A great gale split the oak's thick trunk,
But the reed regained her form.

iv

The King of Sung, being slow to master
The Way, set off — alone —
For help with learning better, faster.
Chuang Tzu sat still as a stone:

"Why bring so many people – who
Are they?" The King looked round
In amazement. "They are and are not you,
Your Highness. To free the bound

(For a king can also be the slave
Of events – or 'human history'),
We must rethink, retell, outbrave
Our own / their / her / his story."

The King went home. To rule he required
Another sort of adviser –
Regretful that one who understood
So much should leave him no wiser.

v

When once again the village chanced
To be embroiled in a war,
The villagers worked – sang – played – and danced,
If anything, more than before.

The Mayor was, frankly, baffled – and, worried,
Publicly blamed Chuang Tzu,
Who (always polite, always unflurried)
Asked, "What would you *like* them to do?"

vi

A monkey trainer, handing out
The monkeys' acorns, told them:
"Three in the morning, four at night."
They shrieked and yelled. To scold them
Would only cause more trouble: "All right –
It's risking my job, but let's say
Four in the morning, three at night."

– The monkeys shouted *Hurray!*

vii

An angry child ran round and round
Trying to chase away
His shadow. Even the clacking sound
Of his clogs made him cry.

A snake hissed, *Come, dear boy – relax,*
And be still in the tranquil shade
Of this tree-of-heaven. No shadow, no clacks.
And no reason to be afraid.

viii

A rich young prince's carriage-driver,
Wishing to impress his master,
Displayed his horse-drawn skills – out-rivalled
His fellows, wheeling faster

And faster, racing straight ahead
And back. Chuang Tzu cried, "Bid
Him stop, sire. Or they'll drop down dead."
But he didn't – and they did.

"How did you know?" the Prince inquired.
– "The horses' strength was gone.
The driver feared as much, but aspired
To excel. And lashed them on."

ix

The same young prince went hunting: a crowd
Of monkeys hid their faces.
Not so their leader – who, loud and proud,
Put on rude airs, crude graces.

He caught the arrows which the Prince
Let fly – snapped each in two.
Ten bowmen aimed and shot. The mince
Made them a right royal stew.

x

A swallowtail settled, and Chuang Tzu dreamed
He *was* the butterfly,
So pleased to be free! When he woke, he seemed
(Without yet knowing why)

To be the fluttering butterfly still,
Dreaming he was Chuang Tzu.
So what was the difference?... Needing to fill
Its belly, a fat toad knew.

xi

Chu'i the draughtsman's mind was easy.
Easy is right. Start right
And you *are* easy. By going easy,
You forget what's easy, what's right.

When your shoes fit you forget your feet;
When your belt fits, your waist.
Chu'i drew circles freehand – complete
And faultless. No effort. No waste.

xii

Chuang Tzu was fishing. The King of Sung
Sent two high-ranking lords
To employ the sharpness of his tongue,
The wisdom of his words.

A turtle dragged its tail in the mud
Of the deep slow river. Another –
Bejewelled, polished, sacred, but dead –
Worshipped, but wired together

With gold – was kept by the King in a heavy
Glass case: "What's bad? What's good?
My lords – decide for yourselves. And leave me
To drag my tail in the mud."

Acknowledgements and Notes

ACKNOWLEDGEMENTS AND NOTES

Opus 1 is the complete first part of *Then and Now*, earlier versions of some sections and notes having appeared in *Then and Now – Words in the Dark* (2002) and *From Now to Then* (2005). These versions – or drafts, as most of them now seem – have been rewritten, rearranged and supplemented by later work to bring the book as a whole (including its format) into line with the third part, *Opus 3*, which was published before it, in 2018. Poems and prose from *Opus 1* have appeared in: *Acumen, Agenda, The Dark Horse, The Fortnightly Review, HQ Magazine, Icta, Modern Poetry in Translation, Orbis, Pennine Platform, Poetry Salzburg Review, Stand, The Rialto*. Sections (1) & (2) of *Aesopean* were published under that title as a pamphlet by Shoestring Press in 2022.

As in previous volumes of *Then and Now*, the 'Acknowledgements and Notes' in *Opus 1* are intended to complement and in places to act as a form of counterpoint to its main text. For these reasons I have done what I could to avoid the sort of academic references to 'further reading' found, for example, in the concluding pages of *The Waste Land;* nor have I commented on everything on which a comment might have been written: *Then and Now* – like life – is nothing if not eclectic. The notes are, of course, subsidiary to the poems and prose which they relate to. Some of them consist of essay-like commentary as much as if not more than background information. Some include poems. The book has been written, even so, to be read like any other annotated text: i.e. the main sections or subsections first (and second or third), since these can for the most part be understood without the notes, which then add to them.

One occasionally encounters the view that in the modern world virtually anyone can look up virtually anything, and this is relevant up to a point. However, it has often enough been said that the Age of Information is one in which ignorance prevails – and there may be more to this than the familiar idea that information is not knowledge (let alone wisdom). Among the disadvantages – seemingly inextricable from the advantages – of the worldwide web is its very size: the bigger it becomes the less we know of it. In *Avatars of the Tortoise* Jorge Luis Borges wrote, "There is a concept which corrupts and upsets all others. I refer not to Evil, whose limited realm is that of ethics; I refer to the infinite." If this is the case (or even if all we are confronted with is an unmanageable vastness), what an author *chooses* to include in / exclude from his work now matters more than ever.

Author's Prologue

p.5, "**this strange disease of modern life**": As long ago as 1853 Matthew Arnold wrote in *The Scholar Gipsy:*

> O born in days when wits were fresh and clear,
> And life ran gaily as the sparkling Thames;
> Before this strange disease of modern life,

>   With its sick hurry, its divided aims,
>   Its heads o'ertaxed, its palsied hearts, was rife –
>   Fly hence, our contact fear!…

Not that flight – or any other form of Romantic withdrawal – has been of much help… Arnold makes a fuller appearance later, in *No.2*, section 5, 'Heine's Grave', while the Scholar Gipsy turns up in the alternative (or concomitant) Romantic mode of self-assertion as Eliot's Coriolan (see *Difficulties of a White-Collar Worker*) – still "waiting for the spark from Heaven to fall", in Arnold's beautiful but useless words…

p.6, **I wonder what you'll make of it**: Cp. Borges' conviction that "a book is more than a verbal structure or series of verbal structures; it is the dialogue it establishes with its reader… This dialogue is infinite… A book is not an isolated being: it is a relationship, an axis of innumerable relationships" *(A Note on (towards) Bernard Shaw)*.

OPUS 1, NO.1: SELF-PORTRAIT AS A WHITE-COLLAR WORKER (1) – FROM HAND TO MOUTH

p.9, ***Difficulties of a White-Collar Worker:*** Cp. T.S. Eliot, *Coriolan* (1931). The poem presumes that the "young Cyril" mentioned in 'Triumphal March' is the son of "Arthur Edward Cyril Parker" in 'Difficulties of a Statesman' and that the "he" (presumably Coriolan) of the first section is also the "I" (presumably the "Statesman") of the second. Shortly before writing *Coriolan*, T.S.E. formulated his well-known description of his "general point of view… as classicist in literature, royalist in politics, and Anglo-Catholic in religion" *(For Lancelot Andrewes*, 1928). In 'The Function of Criticism' (1923) Eliot had characterized – or rather, caricatured – the difference between Classicism and Romanticism as "the difference between the complete and the fragmentary, the adult and the immature, the orderly and the chaotic." Probably not even his harshest critic would want to describe *Old Possum's* poetry as fragmentary, immature and chaotic. Even so, it is now difficult to understand how anyone could have been taken in by his claim to be a "classicist in literature". Eliot seems, however, to have appreciated in general the advantages of having a foot in both camps – starting with America and England. As Peter Ackroyd pointed out in his ground-breaking biography: "Almost from the beginning [he] had a clear understanding of the mechanics of making a literary reputation…" *(T.S. Eliot*, 1984, p.101).

Then and Now also alludes to *The Waste Land* and other works by Eliot. One would hardly guess it from the poem itself but *The Waste Land* seems largely to have been written because of his own difficulties as a white-collar worker – most of it during a three-month break (on doctor's orders) in Margate and then Lausanne in mid-winter 1921–22. In Lausanne he was treated for a nervous breakdown whose immediate cause seems to have been overwork, much of it at Lloyds Bank in the City of London – where his office was across the road from King William Street, "where St Mary Woolnoth kept the hours / With a dead sound on the final stroke of nine" ('The Burial of the Dead', ll.67–68): "A phenomenon which I have often noticed", as he primly (and grimly) noted... **John Quinn** was a New York lawyer and patron of the arts, who was of much assistance to the young Eliot, although they never met. Ezra Pound wrote to the lawyer in June 1920: "No use blinking the fact that it is a crime against literature to let him waste eight hours vitality per diem in that bank." But Eliot wasted his vitality there for altogether eight years, finally leaving Lloyds to join **Faber & Gwyer, publishers** in 1925.

p.10, **"Fool," said my boss to me: "Poetry's a mug's game..."** Etc.: In the first sonnet of the first major sonnet sequence in English – Sir Philip Sidney's *Astrophil and Stella* (1591) – the poet laments his inability to express his love, until its concluding line: " 'Fool,' said my muse to me, 'look in thy heart and write.' " Eliot, however, wrote in *The Use of Poetry and the Use of Criticism* (1933), "The works of Sir Philip Sidney are not among those to which one can return for perpetual refreshment." With hindsight, one might be forgiven for suspecting that at least one of the uses of criticism in the case of T.S.E. was to commend his own *sort* of poetry at the cost of others'. Not that this aspect of the matter could be openly discussed: "I want to boom Eliot," as Pound wrote to John Quinn, "and one cant have too obvious a ping-pong match at that sort of thing." In his 'Conclusion' to *The Use of Poetry and the Use of Criticism* Eliot wrote, "Poetry is not a career, but a mug's game..." His American family – particularly his father – disapproved of his residence in England in order to "mess up his life for nothing", pursuing what turned out in the end, though, to be as successful a career as any careerist could desire.

p.12, *Heinrich Heine: 'Deutschland. Ein Wintermärchen'*: Heine was born in Düsseldorf in 1797 and spent much of his young manhood in Hamburg. Inspired by the July Revolution of 1830, which deposed Charles X, the last Bourbon king, and placed the citizen-king Louis-Philippe on the throne, he moved to Paris in 1831. As early as 1835 Heine's reputation as a radical had become sufficient for the German authorities to ban his writings, and he was to spend the rest of his life in Paris, where he died in 1856... He wrote the more than 500 quatrains of his semi-fictitious 'travel epic', *Deutschland. Ein Wintermärchen* at the beginning of 1844, after spending two months in Germany. This classic of humorous and satirical poetry describes – entertainingly – ambivalently – sadly – some of his experiences while travelling and in various cities, including Hamburg, where he visited his mother and other members of his family, as well as his publisher, Julius Campe. Heine had powerful enemies in Germany by this time, however, and in December 1844 the King of Prussia issued a warrant for his arrest. Even so, Campe managed by one means and another to outwit the authorities and keep Heine's books available.

As regards the translations here and elsewhere in *Self-Portrait as a White-Collar Worker*, these are – as indicated by their context – intended as a variety of quotation on the part of the persona. The poems and prose of which all four parts of the 'sequence-within-the-sequence' also consist (see *Opus 2* and *Opus 3* for Pts (3) and (4) respectively) are similarly presented as *by* the persona as well as 'about' him... The translations elsewhere in *Then and Now* contribute more directly (though still in the form of quotation) to the step-by-step process of creating the 'imaginary identity' to which the work gives rise – of which more below.

p.14, **Hoffmann von F.**: Hoffmann von Fallersleben (1798–1874), a popular poet "dismissed from his Breslau professorship in 1842 for his ironically titled *Unpolitical Songs*. He became for a while the beatnik poet of nineteenth century Germany, travelling from tavern to tavern with his guitar and simple and humorous but biting songs… [Heine] came to abominate [him]: he took Hoffmann as a symptom of the destruction of poesy by democracy, a process in which he considered political poetry to be a transitional phenomenon" (J. L. Sammons, *Heinrich Heine: A Modern Biography*, 1979, p.255). Hoffmann has the dubious distinction of having written the so-called *Deutschlandlied* – *"Deutschland, Deutschland über alles"*.

p.15, **Jandl**, *Aus der Fremde:* Ernst Jandl (1925–2000) was a leading Viennese avant-garde poet – a self-confessed pessimist with a sense of black humour. Sub-sections ii, v, xiv, xviii and xix of *From Hand to Mouth* are adapted from his work. His 'speech-opera' *Aus der Fremde* is, among other things, a portrait of himself attempting to write the very play in which he is the principal character. The dialogue takes place entirely in the third person and in a form of reported speech which can be used to imply hypothesis or unreality. This makes the play practically untranslatable since this sort of subjunctive tense has no reliable equivalent in English. The epigraph, roughly translated, means:

> *(He:)* whether the broken half always had to fall
> with the jam-side down
>
> ever disgustedly did he make use of
> the little hand-brush
>
> trivialities of that kind
> kept jolting into
>
> his very existence!

In spite of its grammatical and other difficulties the play is effective on the stage and ran successfully in Munich, Berlin, Hanover and elsewhere in 1980/1981… In 1945 the nineteen-year-old Jandl was taken prisoner-of-war by the Americans, and translations and adaptations of poems relating to the Second World War are to be found in *Opus 3, No.2*, section 2, iii, 'after jandl'.

p.26, *a tale / Which Phaedrus wrote in verse:* The Latin poet Phaedrus was probably the first, in the early first century AD, to write down some of the fables (in all about 120) traditionally ascribed to Aesop: cp. note on *Aesopean (1)* below… The concluding (italicized) stanzas of section 6 are not a translation but a continuation of Heine's *Das Sklavenschiff*, which was first published in 1854, at a time when (although the trade itself was as good as prohibited) the Kansas-Nebraska Act had caused dismay among abolitionists by permitting the extension of slavery to the American Middle West.

p.28, *The following poem etc.:* The 'Self-portrait as…' does not mention in this note – as if excused from doing so by poetic licence? – the fact that there were not "Twelve" but *four* TVs in Percy Shaw's lounge (to prevent the guests at his frequent house-parties from quarrelling over which channel to watch); that there is no evidence that he collected works of art (let alone locked them up out of sight); that he drank only beer (no more than four pints); that he had probably never been bored in his life; and that he had no children. I have been unable to trace the source of the "ex-champ boxer" with his eighteen Rolls Royces. However, one of the few luxuries Percy Shaw allowed himself was that he owned two.

p.30, "**In the great City pent**": The quotation is from Coleridge's *This Limetree Bower My Prison* (1797), which is addressed to Charles Lamb, who worked as a clerk in London:

> My gentle-hearted Charles! For thou hast pined
> And hunger'd after Nature, many a year,
> In the great City pent, winning thy way
> With sad yet patient soul, through evil and pain
> And strange calamity!

The "strange calamity" presumably refers to the fact that Lamb's sister Mary had murdered their mother Elizabeth with a kitchen knife only the year before. The Lamb family was more than usually afflicted with mental and physical illness, which Coleridge (and Wordsworth?) may well have related to their life in the city… The idea that the countryside is an inherently better and more 'poetic' place to live is still current in one form or another. In the nineteenth century life in the country could perhaps be *pleasanter* and no doubt *healthier*… Eric Hobsbawm, writing in *The Age of Revolution* (1962) of the era's achievements, reminds us as well of "the fact, which few today would deny, that the Industrial Revolution created the ugliest world in which man has ever lived, as the grim and stinking fog-bound backstreets from Manchester to Liverpool already testified. Or, by uprooting men and women in unprecedented numbers and depriving them of the certainties of the ages, probably the unhappiest world" (where generations of my own forebears lived and died, incidentally).

Aesopean (1)

p.39, *"Aesop the storyteller etc.":* The historical Aesop may well have been a Greek-speaking slave, later freedman, living in Phrygia in the fifth or sixth century BC. Apart from a number of anonymous pre-Christian Greek collections, many of the fables as we know them were first written down by Greek and Latin authors and others (notably the Augustan poet Phaedrus, who may also have been a slave and then freedman) from the first century AD onwards. Editions and translations are many and various – some of them adaptations of 'originals' which may themselves be adaptations of still earlier versions unknown to us. It is only in a limited sense, therefore, that short tales of this sort – whose roots and ramifications are practically endless –

can be viewed as the work of a particular author: the latest version is no more, or less, than the latest version. A sizeable group of earlier fables might be thought of, even so, as displaying a clever slave's mentality, perhaps Aesop's own: realistic, pragmatic, amoral to the point of heartless – with little or no interest in "whatever it means to be *free*" *(No.2*, section 5, p.78), which only a fool, according to this view of things, would seek to become. Be this as it may, most fables are practically anonymous. As for the genre as a whole, it always has been and presumably always will be with us.

p.42, *(after Grimms' Märchen, No.75):* The famous collection of folktales by Jakob and Wilhelm Grimm, *Kinder- und Haus-Märchen* (1812–14 / 1857), includes a number of Aesopean fables. Other tales from the Grimms' collection are adapted elsewhere in *Then and Now:* cp. headnote to *No.3*, section 6, 'The Bride's Story' (p.150).

Opus 1, No.2: Self-Portrait as a White-Collar Worker (2) – Words in the Dark

p.45, **Self-Portrait as a White-Collar Worker** (2): As noted above, the poems, prose and translations/quotations of which *Self-Portrait as a White-Collar Worker* consists are (of course) to be understood as *by* the persona as well as 'about' him, whose identity is thus built up – in fact develops – as time goes on (in Pt (2) *ca.* 6–7 years) and as the events of his life affect him… As common in painting as it is in literature, the 'self-portrait as …' is, potentially, a more fanciful and also, from an ethical viewpoint, more complex genre than the straight self-portrait; and many artists and writers from Botticelli to Picasso and from Chaucer to James Joyce have exploited its double-edged capacity for appraising a) the role in question and b) themselves as if playing it. Thus Botticelli paints himself as an arrogant hanger-on in *The Adoration of the Magi* (*ca.* 1475); Titian as King Midas in *The Flaying of Marsyas* (1570); and Rembrandt as a drunken Prodigal Son toasting the viewer (1638). In other examples of the genre the artist may or may not have played the role in question in actual life. Chaucer may in fact have been a Canterbury pilgrim – though scarcely one so incapable of telling an interesting tale in decent verse that the Host has to cut him off (see 'Chaucers Tale of Thopas' in *The Canterbury Tales).* Although Joyce was in fact a bohemian *Artist,* a Dubliner, and at one time *a Young Man,* many aspects of his *[Self-] Portrait as…* – which continues into *Ulysses* – are obviously fictional. Similarly, Pts (1) & (2) of the sequence are set in England in the 1980s, whereas *I* have lived in Italy and, for the most part, Germany since 1972… However, as Borges was fond of pointing out, even an "I" such as this is a more or less conscious – more or less deliberate – construct on the part of a real person, the author. His favourite illustration of this fact (as it seems to be) was the difference between what is known of the real person, Walt Whitman, and the "Walt Whitman" of *Leaves of Grass.* In two essays, for example, in *Other Inquisitions* (trans. 1964), Borges discusses "the fact that there are two Whitmans, the 'friendly and eloquent savage' of *Leaves of Grass* and the poor writer who invented him". That is: "Whitman wrote his rhapsodies in terms of an imaginary identity formed partly of himself, partly of each of his readers. Hence the discrepancies which have exasperated the critics; hence the custom of dating his poems in places where he had never been; hence the fact that, on one page of his work, he was born in the Southern states and, on another (and also in reality) on Long Island" – and so on. In the eloquent hall-of-mirrors which is 'Borges and I' (*Labyrinths*, pp.282–284), "The other one" – the one who contrives his literature, "falsifying and magnifying things", he tells us – "is the one things happen to" .. From this to the famous paradox of Shakespeare's most realistic Fool – that "...the truest poetry is the most feigning" (*As You Like It*, III.iii.16) – is no big step. But, whether one takes it or declines it, the author in the real world clearly has some choice in the matter of how he represents both the world and himself: "A false fact may be essentially true", Borges states – as Shakespeare also knew when in his history plays he adapted history itself to suit what he wanted to say.

p.47, ***"Doubt thou the stars are fire, etc."***: The poem presumes (*pace* the Arden *Hamlet*, 1982) that Hamlet knew very well that it was now doubtful whether the sun moved and was therefore fully aware of the ironies with which his letter to Ophelia is fraught.

p.48, **"The new Philosophy calls all in doubt; etc."**: Three lines from *An Anatomie of the World – The First Anniversary* (1611). Donne's great poem, hyperbolically inverting *Genesis* by attributing the fallen and disintegrating state of our world to the departure from it of a superlatively good and beautiful woman – not a 'real' woman, as he told Ben Jonson, but the Idea of one – includes the discoveries of Copernicus and Galileo as one of the causes and/or symptoms of its increasing decadence and disunity (ll.199–238):

> 'Tis all in pieces, all cohaerence gone;
> All just supply, and all Relation...
> This is the worlds condition now, and now
> She that should all parts to reunion bow,
> She that had all Magnetique force alone,
> To draw, and fasten sundred parts in one;...
> Shee, shee is dead; she's dead: when thou know'st this,
> Thou know'st how lame a cripple this world is.

The four hundred years which separate us from Donne's poem have been years of science and technology, capitalism, worldwide imperialism, wars of unimaginable magnitude and (increasingly) pollution. Donne implied that there are certain (female) virtues which might still help us – but feared that it was already too late.

An Anatomie of the World is mentioned in a related context by Borges in his essay, *The Fearful Sphere of Pascal* (1951), in which he offers an account of "that dispirited century", the seventeenth, which concentrates on Pascal's *Pensées:* "The absolute space which had meant liberation to Bruno became a labyrinth and an abyss to Pascal... He felt the incessant weight of the physical world...". According to Borges, "...men felt lost in time and space. In time, because if the future and the past are infinite, there cannot really be a when; in space, because if every being is equidistant from the infinite and infinitesimal, neither can there be a where." He might have added that men must have felt even more lost whenever they thought of the new universe, as Pascal thought of it, in relationship to the old idea of God's omniscient omnipotence:

> When I consider the brief span of my life absorbed into the eternity which comes before and after – "as the remembrance of a guest that tarrieth but a day" – the small space I occupy and which I see swallowed up in the infinite immensity of spaces of which I know nothing and which know nothing of me, I take fright and am amazed to see myself here rather than there: there is no reason for me to be here rather than there, *now* rather than *then*. Who put me here? By whose command and act were this time and place allotted to me? *(Pensées 68)*

As long as there was such a God, in other words, the events which ruled our lives were "fearful" indeed. No wonder then that Pascal "experienced vertigo, fright and solitude." Or that "he compared our life with that of castaways on a desert island…".

In contrast with Borges' attempt to sketch a chapter – as he puts it himself – of "universal history", Eliot misleadingly argues in *The Pensées of Blaise Pascal* (1931) that "although Pascal brings to his work the same powers which he exerted in science, it is not as a scientist that he presents himself". Published in the same year as *Coriolan*, Eliot's essay on Pascal is characteristically limited by its author's unwillingness (or inability) to view Christianity historically and by his outdated and conservative persona of Christian apologist. Such a persona might have been viewed by Borges as an opportunity for the "deliberate anachronism" which he discusses in *Pierre Menard, Author of 'Don Quixote'*, and of which Eliot in fact makes effective use in *Coriolan* and elsewhere. But the Eliot of the prose was not the Eliot of the poetry, and his essay is little more than an Anglo-Catholic (and Anglo-American) sermon, exemplifying one of his least appealing solutions to the problem – social and psychological, rather than aesthetic – of how to assert oneself as a poet/outsider who may seem to be "messing up his life for nothing" (cp. end of note on p.10, "'Fool,' said my boss to me: etc.").

p.48, **Now that our world has been relieved / … Of nicely explained religion**: At the end of Brecht's *Leben des Galilei* (1938/1939), Galileo regrets the bad example he has set to scientists by giving in to and appearing to work for authority (i.e. the Roman Catholic Church) after his recantation to the Inquisition of his most important discoveries – although his pupil Andrea rejoices at what he takes to be a subterfuge whereby Galileo has completed his work in secret (it was then smuggled out of Italy and published in Holland). It seems not to have occurred to Brecht's Marxist-materialist mind (even in his later revisions of the play, after Hiroshima) that the scientific way of thinking in itself may conceal as many disadvantages as it has advantages, and that superficial rationalism may be one of the 'original sins' (together with greed, self-interest, self-importance, and the desire for revenge) which could lead us as a species into even more evolutionary dead-ends than we have entered already. Of course, there are spiritual as well as material 'disadvantages', and in some ways Pascal (1623–1662) saw further than Galileo (1564–1642), even as a scientist. As regards the question of proof, for example, with which Pascal – as a mathematician and technologist – was as obsessed as anyone, *Pensées* 521 observes:

It may be that there are such things as true proofs, but it is not certain.

Thus this only proves that it is not certain that everything is uncertain.
To the greater glory of scepticism.

O brave new world!… But Pascal derived comfort as well from the fact that "We know the truth not only through our reason but also through our heart" *(Pensées* 110). Or, more famously, that "The heart has its reasons of which reason knows nothing" (423)…

p.52, **The 1st of May comes in etc.**: In some respects the poems in *Forms of Fall* are expressions of Heine's struggle to de-Romanticize his poetry, as well as of his thoughts and feelings *re* the larger themes with which they engage. This can perhaps be more clearly seen by comparing them with a simpler poem more obviously probing the poet's own Romantic tendencies:

The Old Chimney-Corner

Out-of-doors white flakes are blowing
Through the night; the storm is loud;
But the kitchen fire is glowing
Far from any town or crowd.

By the crackling fire I settle,
Warm and dry in my favourite chair,
Lost in thought; the boiling kettle
Hums a long-forgotten air,

While a little cat sits playing –
Warms her paws beside the fire;
And the fire-light's weaving, swaying,
Fills my heart with strange desire…

Long-forgotten springs and summers
Dawn and come to life again,
Bringing coloured masks and mummers –
Faded splendour – gentlemen

Whose sweet ladies' knowing glances
Beckon enigmatically;
Harlequin cavorts and prances,
Laughing with unruly glee.

Farther off great gods of marble
Greet us; near them flowers grow

> Dreamily, as in a fable;
> Moonlit leaves wave to and fro.
>
> Old enchanted castles, gliding
> Waterily, wobble by;
> Knights-at-arms come palely riding,
> Leading page and pageantry...
>
> But these visions fade forever,
> Over-hasty, fast as dreams. –
> Now the kettle's boiling over,
> And the scalded kitten screams!

On the other hand, the relationship between this sort of poem and those in *Forms of Fall* could also be taken to imply that the difference between Romantic and post-Romantic ways of seeing (and saying) things is as large a theme as any... In poems such as *Deutschland. Ein Wintermärchen* or *Das Sklavenschiff*, and in his later work generally, Heine achieved his own sort of fully developed realism.

p.55, **With chaste Judaic-Christian fig-leaf pinnies**: Heine was born into a Jewish family, converting to Lutheranism in 1825. His conversion was largely for practical reasons, however – Jews had limited rights in nineteenth century Germany – and he wrote much prose and many poems on Jewish themes. Heine's feelings with regard to the history and practice of Judaism, as well as to his apostasy, were rarely simple (cp. 'Adam the First' in this section, or 'Three Poems on the History of Religion' in *Opus 3, No.1*), but he expresses them with characteristic honesty, intelligence and wit – as when, in the beautiful *Jehuda ben Halevy*, he identifies with the Jewish poets of medieval Spain, presenting them, and also himself (in what has been called "a complex act of self-affirmation"), as typical members of "the House of Schlemiel"...

p.56, **I was the man / Who lay there dead**: For the last eight years of his life (from 1848 to 1856) Heine was painfully and increasingly paralysed by a disease of the spinal cord which confined him to what he referred to in his writings as his *"Matratzengruft"* (mattress-grave). The pain was relieved by dripping morphine into wounds kept open for this purpose on his back, but he suffered badly from cramps, bed-sores and sleeplessness as well as from the ravages of his illness. He was also chronically short of money, having lived for virtually his entire working life from his writings. And yet by common consent Heine composed some of his finest poetry during this period. He was looked after by his devoted but almost illiterate French wife, Mathilde. Shortly before the end, however, he fell in love with a mysterious young visitor, whom he nicknamed *"die Mouche"* (the fly). *"Es träumte mir von einer Sommernacht"* is sometimes known as *Für die Mouche*.

p.59, ***"Pleasure ... generates submission"***: In ch.3 of *One-Dimensional Man* Marcuse argues that in our late capitalist or advanced industrial civilization, "the status quo [is one] of general repression" which apparent or superficial freedoms (as in the so-called 'permissive society' of the 1960s) not only fail to oppose but in practice help to preserve. In other words, "the social controls of technological reality extend liberty while intensifying domination." Only twenty years after the Second World War, it was possible for Marcuse to write: "If mass communications blend together harmoniously, and often unnoticeably, art, politics, religion and philosophy with commercials" in the all-pervading commercialization of society, "they bring these realms of culture down to their common denominator – the commodity form. The music of the soul is also the music of salesmanship. Exchange value, not truth value counts." In this view of things, the tendency of post-War art to conform with such developments – its failure to create another dimension by standing over against them – means that "The achievements and failures of this society invalidate its higher culture." The very real danger of such cultural pollution becomes clearer as time goes on. On the other hand, the Russian émigré poet, Joseph Brodsky, whose poetry had been denounced as "pornographic and anti-Soviet", who had been twice confined to a mental institution, charged with "social parasitism" and sentenced to hard labour in Siberia before being exiled in 1971, was fond of pronouncements such as "Basically, talent has no need of history" or "Art is not an attempt to escape reality but … to animate it." Of which more in *Opus 3*.

p.64, **These crossed-out lines of Keats**: The epigraph is from a passage in *The Fall of Hyperion* (Canto I, ll.187–210) which, although it is included in most modern editions, Keats seems to have cancelled. This cancellation may well have reflected some temporary indecision on the ailing Keats's part as to whether poetry is of any value or use whatever in the modern world: is it not all mere "dreaming", as the passage preceding the cancellation seems to imply…?

p.64, **As the law might take for 'loitering'**: The notorious 'sus' law allowed the police to stop, search and even arrest "'suspected persons' and 'reputed thieves' who 'frequent and loiter' in certain public places with intent to commit an arrestable offence" (quoted in *OED)*. The law (based on the Vagrancy Act of 1824) was increasingly used – and resented – in the 1970s in Britain's inner cities (for example, almost 4,000 people were stopped and searched, and 180 of them arrested, on Merseyside alone between January and July 1981) and was a major cause of rioting in Toxteth, Bristol, Brixham and elsewhere at the time. In August 1981 the law was repealed.

p.64, **"How right the workers are,"** etc.: Slightly adapted from the concluding section of George Orwell's essay, *Looking Back on the Spanish War* (1943), written while he was living in London and working for the BBC. Orwell's view that there could be as good as no spiritual life without an "indispensable minimum" of *material* well-being ("enough to eat, freedom from the haunting terror of unemployment, the knowledge that your children will get a fair chance, a bath once a day [!], clean linen reasonably often, a roof that doesn't leak, and short enough working hours to leave you with a little energy when the day is done") is still true of most people – although his knowledge of the working class and its supposed "decency" remained that of an outside observer. If it was true up to a point that "behind all the ballyhoo that is talked about the 'materialism' of the working class lies the simple intention of those with money or privileges to cling to them", the new white-collar 'working class' which, amid widespread affluence, now dominates the Western world is quite clearly *as* 'materialistic' and probably more so. As Brodsky, with his first-hand experience of both Communism *and* capitalism, might have written, materialism (or greed) of this sort appears to be less a "political problem" than "a human problem, a problem of our species, and thus of a lingering nature" ('Letter to a President' in *On Grief and Reason*). In the same open letter, addressed to Vaclav Havel in 1993, Brodsky wrote: "Why don't we simply start by admitting that an extraordinary anthropological backslide has taken place in our world in this century, regardless of who or what triggered it? That it involved masses acting in their self-interest and, in the process of doing so, reducing their common denominator to the moral minimum? And that the masses' self-interest – stability of life and its standards, similarly reduced – has been attained at the expense of other masses, albeit numerically inferior?"

p.69, **But its creator / Knew it might change the world**: Cp. Brodsky: "Now, the purpose of evolution is the survival neither of the fittest nor of the defeatist… The purpose of evolution, believe it or not, is beauty, which survives it all and generates truth simply by being a fusion of the mental and the sensual" ('An Immodest Proposal' in *On Grief and Reason*). On the other hand, "There are few cures for hereditary disorders (undetectable, perhaps, in an individual, but striking in a crowd), and what I'm suggesting here is not one of them… The fact that we are alive does not mean that we are not sick" *(ibid)*.

p.70, **In Lieu of a Manifesto: Heine's Grave:** Five stanzas of this poem (from "Rightly he feared us!" to *"pereat mundus!"*) consist largely of an adaptation into Arnoldian verse of a famous passage from Heine's preface to *Lutèce* (1855), the French edition of *Lutezia*, a collection of articles about the life and culture of Paris written mainly for a leading German newspaper, the *Augsburger Allgemeine*. The poem also quotes and adapts from Brodsky's 'A Commencement Address' (in *Less Than One*) and Matthew Arnold's poems *Heine's Grave, The Scholar Gipsy, Lines Written in Kensington Gardens, Memorial Verses* and *Obermann Once More*. Arnold wrote an outstanding appreciation of Heine – first delivered as a lecture at Oxford in 1863, where he was pleased, as he wrote in a letter, that "even a wooden Oxford audience … positively laughed aloud" at his examples of Heine's wit. Arnold wrote as a poet ("The magic of Heine's poetical form is incomparable") and as a historian of ideas and critic of contemporary culture. In spite of his admiration for Heine's "intense modernism, his absolute freedom, his utter rejection of stock classicism and stock romanticism", however, and in spite as well of his awareness that in comparison the works of the English Romantics "have this defect: they do not belong to that which is the main current of the literature of modern epochs, they do not apply modern ideas to life", Arnold concluded: "He died and has left a blemished name; with his crying faults – his intemperate susceptibility, his unscrupulousness in passion, his inconceivable attacks on his enemies, his still more inconceivable attacks on his friends, his want of generosity, his sensuality, his incessant mocking – how could it be otherwise? Not only was he not one of Mr Carlyle's 'respectable' people, he was profoundly *dis*respectable; and not even the merit of not being a Philistine can make up for a man's being that… Heine had all the culture of Germany; in his head fermented all the ideas of modern Europe. And what have we got from Heine? A half-result, for want of moral balance, and of nobleness of soul and character" *(Essays in Criticism)*.

p.71, **better than Marx**: Heine became friendly with Karl Marx in 1844 while the latter was living in Paris. According to one anecdote, which may or may not be apocryphal, Heine was one day visiting the Marxes when their daughter Jenny began to choke. In the ensuing panic it was Heine who saved the child's life by turning her upside down and slapping her back until the morsel of food was dislodged. He later recommended that Marx should spend more time reading the Bible. By this he presumably meant that, although Marx was learned in philosophy and economics, he didn't know enough about people.

p.79, **He got a job and married**: In 1851 Arnold was appointed to an inspectorship of schools, a post which enabled him to marry and which he held for thirty-five years. Most of his best-known poetry had been written before this time. Heine, on the other hand, tended to align himself in his writings with society's outsiders and even outcasts. In his youth he might have become a businessman but displayed little interest and less talent – even with the backing of his immensely rich uncle, Salomon Heine, one of the most successful bankers in the country. He then laboriously studied law – at the universities of Bonn, Göttingen and Berlin – and graduated with a doctorate in 1825. Unlike Arnold, though, who became Professor of Poetry at Oxford, Heine had little time for nineteenth century academicism – particularly after the failure of his (somewhat half-hearted) efforts to become Professor of Poetry at Munich University in 1828. This was almost certainly because of intrigue on the part of a Bavarian Catholic faction, but also because of what many already saw as the scurrility, if not obscenity, of his writings – as both exemplified and humorously flaunted in *Buch der Lieder,* which had been published the year before:

Die Heimkehr LXXIX

>The *castrati* started complaining
>When I began to huff –
>Complaining and explaining
>My voice was much too gruff.
>
>Their little voices, trilling
>In chorus, rose as clear
>As crystal. O how thrilling
>To sound so truly pure!
>
>They sang of love effusively,
>Of desire beyond all measure;
>The ladies wept profusely
>At such aesthetic pleasure.

It can hardly have helped his chances in Munich that Heine also said what he thought of academics unfortunate enough to have displeased him. One of his snubs (quoted by Arnold in *Essays in Criticism*) was to lament the dreadful fate which had been suffered by all three of Napoleon's greatest opponents: Castlereagh had cut his own throat, Louis XVIII had rotted upon his throne – and Professor Saalfeld was still a professor at Göttingen! Elsewhere in *Buch der Lieder* (in *Die Heimkehr* LVIII) he had written:

> This world and this life are just too fragmented:
> I'm off to the German Prof. who's invented
> A system for putting them back together
> That's as clear as beer. With nothing worse
> Than his nightgown and other bedroom clobber
> He's stopped up the gaps in the universe.

As well as a doctor of law, Heine had become a Lutheran in 1825 (cp. note on p.55, "With chaste Judaic-Christian fig-leaf pinnies"), but he made no further use of these certificates after leaving Munich, preferring to live by his writing. He had started publishing in 1822, and *Buch der Lieder* (1827) was a collection of his earlier poetry, consisting of 237 poems in all. The book was a success and for a time Heine became something of a social celebrity. His view of such matters was typically ambivalent if not jaundiced, however – as in *Die Heimkehr* LXV, one of his *Doppelgänger* poems:

> Such a fine young man, delighting
>   All who have the luck to meet him.
> Oysters, Rhenish and liqueurs he
>   Treats me to, though I don't treat him.
>
> Smart he looks in pants and jacket,
>   Smarter still his silk cravat.
> – In he sidles every morning:
>   Am I well enough to chat?
>
> Tells me how my reputation
>   Grows apace – for charm *and* wit;
> While he, active in my interest,
>   Cultivates and nurtures it.
>
> Evenings, in the social whirl,
>   He enthuses soulfully –
> Charms the ladies by performing
>   My divine love poetry…

> Well, it's certainly rewarding
> To discover such a youth
> In our time: the better sort is
> Dying out – and that's the truth.

p.80, In earlier times they might have burned / Me and my books: In two famous lines from his early verse-play *Almansor* (1823), Heine wrote: *"…dort wo man Bücher verbrennt, / Verbrennt man auch am Ende Menschen"* (where they burn books / In the end they'll burn people) – words now inscribed on German monuments in memory of the one hundred-and-two bonfires of books (including, of course, Heine's own) officially sanctioned in German cities throughout May 1933. At an anti-Semitic (and anti-French) rally in Wartburg in 1817 books had been burned whose authors were considered hostile to the unification of Germany, and Heine would doubtless have known of this. The extraordinary gift or knack whereby Heine was able to foresee social and political developments far beyond his own time has already been exemplified in the passage from *Lutèce* referred to above, in which he saw more accurately than Marx into the future of capitalism. Another famous passage, at the end of *On the History of Religion and Philosophy in Germany* (1835) – written largely for the benefit of French readers – is related to what he says in *Lutèce* of the grocers who will turn his poetry books into bags for their wares: namely, when the German people claim the material well-being which their rulers have tried to deny them, this will be because of – and will also exacerbate – a violent revolt of materialistic/sensual values against spiritual/religious values of any sort:

> Thought precedes action as lightning precedes thunder. German thunder, of course, is not very agile, and rolls along slowly; but it will arrive in due course, and when you hear such a crash as has never yet been heard in the history of the world, you will know that German thunder has reached its goal. When its sound is heard, … a play will be performed in Germany compared with which the French Revolution will seem an inoffensive idyll. At present, indeed, there are only little dogs running around in the empty arena, barking and snapping at each other – until the moment comes for a host of gladiators to arrive and fight to the death. And that moment will come.

Heine's exceptionally wide-ranging and realistic understanding of history from a personal as well as social and political point of view is everywhere apparent not only in his prose but in his poetry, relating poems such as *Götterdämmerung*, for example – with its specifically atavistic ending – or, somewhat differently, *Für die Mouche*, to predictions such as this one, and testifying to the rare integrity or wholeness of Heine's vision, a wholeness which (not surprisingly) also expressed itself in his life.

p.86, "Herwegh, you iron lark!": Georg Herwegh (1817–1875) was a guitar-toting poet and militant radical – the instrument being as popular then as now, apparently. Heine regarded simple-minded socialism with almost as much mistrust as German nationalism and wrote this poem, which he handed to Herwegh personally, after the popular success of the latter's *Gedichte eines Lebendigen (Poems of a Living Man)* in 1841.

Aesopean (2)

p.95, *"a rat is not an elephant"*: In La Fontaine's fable *(ca.* 1678) a rat mocks a majestic elephant, bearing along a Queen with her cat, dog and other accoutrements. The rat asks why observers should praise mere *size*. Marianne Moore, in her superlative *The Fables of La Fontaine* (1952), translates:

> 'Who cares how much space something occupies?'
> He said. 'Size does not make a thing significant!
> All crowding near an elephant? Why must I worship him?
> Servile to brute force at which mere tots might faint?
> Should persons such as I admire his heavy limb?
>   I pander to an elephant!'
>   About to prolong his soliloquy
>   When the cat broke from captivity
>   And instantly proved what her victim would grant:
>   That a rat is not an elephant.

p.95, *(after Lessing):* The pre-Romantic dramatist, poet and critic, G.E. Lessing (1729–81) based most of his mainly prose fables on early Greek and Latin authors such as Aelian and Phaedrus, whose common sense appealed to his Enlightenment values (cp. his tale of the rings in *An East / West Epilogue*, section 2, 'Nathan the Wise – A Medley'). Goethe's and Heine's contributions to the Aesopean tradition (as in *Aesopean (1)*, viii, xi, xii, and *(2)*,v) came somewhat later. Both poets suffered in their earlier work from Romantic attitudes – from which they may be said to have recovered in different ways. A group of fables by Heine (including the original of *(1)*, xii) seems to have been among his last poems, and was published posthumously along with other outstanding work.

p.99, **A badly treated slave complained / To Aesop**: In Phaedrus' version of this fable, Aesop advises the slave to stay where he is, for fear of worse… The free-thinking Borges was at first bored by fables. By 1941, though, he had realized to his growing dismay that "we are *in* the rudimentary world of the slave Aesop" – that the "irrevocably banal" notion of the Third Reich's ambition to conquer the world was not a "deplorable German fable" but in process of becoming real; that we had made no progress: that "men fulminated against by Juvenal rule the destinies of the world."

p.99, *(after Tommaso da Celano):* Tommaso completed the earliest life of the saint in 1229. He certainly knew St Francis in person, becoming a Franciscan monk in 1215, shortly after the order was founded. Ch. XXI is entitled 'Of his preaching to the birds and of the obedience of the creatures'. Other stories of Francis resemble Aesopean fables – for example, St Francis and the cicada (cp. *Aesopean (1)*, v), also from da Celano's book, or 'How St Francis converted the very fierce wolf of Gubbio' *(The Little Flowers of St Francis*, ch. XXI): cp. *Opus 3, No.3*, section 2,

'*Al Vescovo d'Assisi*'. The second and third stanzas of xii are adapted from St Francis' famous 'Canticle of Brother Sun': cp. *Opus 3, No.1*, section 1, 'A Giotto Triptych'.

OPUS 1, NO.3: INTERPRETATIONS

p.101, ***Man is the only being by whom a destruction can be accomplished..., etc.:*** In this (intentionally provocative?) passage, Sartre is discussing more than 'natural catastrophes', of course. In the end he is only saying what is often forgotten, however – that there is no perception without a perceiver, no observation without an observer. Without a perceiver or observer – or "witness", as Sartre says – there is (or would be) no more and no less than what he calls 'being-in-itself', or unconscious matter. "The world is human," as he puts it elsewhere: "We can see the very particular position of consciousness: being is everywhere, opposite me, around me... I want to grasp this being and I no longer find anything but *myself*" (II.3.*V*). *Being and Nothingness* has been described by readers more knowledgeable than I am as the most important book of twentieth century philosophy. Even so – and despite the fact that one of its main subjects is the nature of the relationship between the conscious (human) 'being-for-itself' and the 'in-itself' (II.3.*I*) – the book as a whole evinces remarkably little self-awareness, or understanding in an *everyday* sense of why it is how it is, and what that implies. It is no idle question, in this regard, to ask why he did not write, "man is the only being by whom a *construction* can be accomplished..., etc." One reason worth consideration might have been that the book was first published in German-occupied Paris in 1943. But there may well have been others not irrelevant to Sartre's views on the nature of being and freedom – for example, that we are *"condemned* to freedom" *(Being and Nothingness*, IV.1.*II),* or that, when no particular pain or pleasure occupies the for-itself, its perpetual apprehension of the body is more or less *nauseous*: "A dull and inescapable nausea perpetually reveals my body to my consciousness" (III.2.*I*, concluding paragraph). As *Hamlet* incomparably illustrates, the failure to understand *why* one sees things as one does – and to realize, as far as may be, the freedom of one's choices – tends in itself to 'accomplish' a destruction. *"And yet, and yet..."*, (to employ a phrase of Borges' to which the Borges authority Professor Rogério de Almeida devoted an entire essay – cp. note on p.197, "Chuang Tzu dreamed..."), *Being and Nothingness* remains one of those few great self-contained works which can transform their reader's world.

p.103, ***a garden of fruit-trees and roses:*** Cp. *Hamlet,* I.v.59 ff.:

> Sleeping within my orchard,
> ... Upon my secure hour thy uncle stole
> With juice of cursed hebanon in a vial...

The Ghost's claim that he had been "Cut off even in the blossoms of my sin" (line 76) is later repeated by Hamlet himself when he discovers his uncle praying: "He took my father... / With all his crimes broad blown, as flush as May" (III.iii.80–81). Other details from Shakespeare's play are adapted in one way and another into *Hamlet in England.* When the Player Queen, in 'The

Murder of Gonzago' ("written in very choice Italian" and adapted by Hamlet himself) promises her husband not to re-marry after his death, he responds:

> *Purpose is but the slave to memory,*
> *Of violent birth but poor validity,*
> *Which now, like fruit unripe, sticks on the tree,*
> *But fall unshaken when they mellow be.*
> — III.ii.183–186

By "violent" the King here means passionate, and his simile recalls the Garden of Eden… As for the **roses** (emblems of ideal love), when Hamlet confronts his mother in her bedroom shortly after the play-within-the-play and she asks him "What have I done, that thou dar'st wag thy tongue so rudely against me?" he answers "an act / That

> takes off the rose
> From the fair forehead of an innocent love
> And sets a blister there…
> — III.iv.40–44

p.103, **But I / Too often see / In my mind's eye etc.**: Quoted from *Hamlet*, I.ii.185. A number of parallels are drawn in the poem between Elsinore and "Affrontenburg", which was Heine's name for the country seat of his uncle Salomon, who "at his death must have been one of the wealthiest commoners in all of Germany" (J.L. Sammons, *op cit*). Heine had spent much time at "Affrontenburg", and had even fallen in love with his uncle's daughter, Amalie. In 1827 Salomon financed a trip to England but Heine found the English a prosaic and conservative people – "disagreeable robots, machines whose internal mainspring is egotism" and whose life and character seemed pervaded by the commercial spirit which he abhorred regardless of where he found it. Nevertheless, he addressed a number of poems to a certain "Kitty Clairmont", who must have pleased him somewhat better… Salomon was a *parvenu* and a philistine: Heine's literary activities displeased him (he said if he could *do* anything he wouldn't have to write books) and, although he supported his nephew grudgingly, the poet was more or less permanently short of money. Moreover, the story has recently been unearthed (cp. Sammons, pp.48–50) of how Uncle Salomon ruthlessly and systematically ruined his own brother Samson, Heine's father, thereby hastening Samson's death. The success of uncle and nephew in such different fields – and with such different ideas of what "success" might mean – only exacerbated their frustration with one another: Heine told Salomon that "the best thing about you is that you bear my name" – and Salomon never forgot or forgave it. After the death of his uncle, Heine's cousin Carl made it clear that if he published anything attacking Salomon or Carl's family, his allowance would stop immediately. Even so, Heine published *Affrontenburg* in 1854 (two years before he died). By naming no one, its "Aesopian language" (S.S. Prawer, *Heine's Jewish Comedy*, 1983), was in itself a provocation, whose subject would "easily be recognized by those who knew anything at all of Heine's life history".

The German text of Heine's *Affrontenburg* is available with a literal prose translation in Peter

Branscombe's excellent Penguin selection of the poetry (1967). In the process of freeing himself from his own as well as the age's Romanticism (in his late autobiographical prose-work, *Geständnisse* (1854), he described himself as an *"entlaufener Romantiker"* – an escaped Romantic), Heine devoted a good deal of creative energy to investigating and questioning the nature of imagination and of belief. In this respect, as well as in others, he is a Hamlet-like figure and the Hamlet of this poem (as well as quoting, of course, from *Hamlet*) adapts and quotes from 'Castle Contumely', as Branscombe calls it, and from another well-known poem of this sort, *"Ein Fichtenbaum steht einsam"* (translated above as *Aesopean (2)*,v).

p.107, ***Then a green spookiness etc.:*** The last five stanzas of Heine's *Affrontenburg* are here quoted in translation. *Affrontenburg* is, obviously, a hate poem – on the self-destructive uselessness of hate. Lines from the preceding twelve stanzas have been adapted into *Hamlet in England* up to this point. These stanzas could be translated more exactly as follows (as could the thirteenth, although the version in the main text seemed preferable there):

> Time passes, but *Affrontenburg*
> Still sticks in my mind. At times for hours
> I see its foolish human brutes,
> Its pseudo-Gothic turrets and towers.
>
> I hear the rusty weathercock
> Which creaked on its roof. Ambitious minions
> Would sneak a timid glance up there
> Before considering their opinions.
>
> Whoever spoke there checked which way
> The wind was blowing pretty precisely,
> For fear the old bear, Boreas,
> Might snort at them not very nicely.
>
> In fact, the cleverest kept quite mum:
> An echo in that court distorted
> With malice aforethought every word
> Of gossip which it misreported.
>
> Down in the castle-garden stood
> A marble fountain, ornamented
> With sphinxes, which was always dry
> Except for when my feelings vented

Themselves in tears. I curse that garden! –
There can't have been a single place
In which my heart had not been wrung
Or tears of anger wet my face.

There really can't have been a tree
Beneath which I'd not been insulted
By softer tongues and rougher ones,
And softer / rougher hurt resulted.

The toad, eavesdropping in the grass,
Croaked every word (and more) to the rat,
Who told her aunt, the viper, all
She'd heard / not heard of this and that.

The viper told her brother-in-law,
The frog. And so they hissed / croaked / grunted,
That filthy tribe, the latest news
Of how and where I'd been affronted.

The roses there were beautiful;
A sweet alluring perfume filled them.
But soon they wilted, and soon died:
A mysterious poison killed them.

Also, the nightingale, which sang
For *my* beloved sweet sick rose,
Grew sick itself – and died – from inhaling
The same strange poison, I suppose.

Accursed place! It was as if
A curse in fact was on it. Most
Scarily by the light of day,
I sometimes thought I'd seen a ghost.

As if a spooky greenness grinned
At me, or seemed insanely scoffing –
While out of a squat yew-tree came
A death-like moaning, gasping, coughing…

Etc.

p.109, **the forking paths**: In one of Borges' most labyrinthine stories, *The Garden of Forking Paths,* there is a mysterious novel of that name whose time-scheme is based on the idea that whenever its characters are faced with alternatives they may and do choose both, so that the narrative divides into strands (or "paths") along which the one person simultaneously creates various futures, which also fork – and so on.

p.112, *"Suppose I try to be your mirror"*: Sartre's profoundly original and disturbing play takes place in a room with no windows or mirrors, which its three occupants (who remember their deaths) presume is Hell. One of them remarks, "When I can't see myself I begin to wonder if I really exist". At first polite, they begin tormenting one another and themselves by asking questions, confessing their misdeeds and attempting to dominate or threaten the others or actively reduce them to objects – as the Sartre of *Being and Nothingness* (III.1.*IV,* 'The Look') thought people always do. This leads, by the end of the play, to the famous Existentialist slogan, "Hell is other people."

p.116, *A King and Not a King:* An adaptation of one of Aesop/Phaedrus' cleverest fables, which has been interpreted in various ways. The epigraph from La Fontaine consists of the first two lines of his version, 'The Frogs Ask for a King', which was written shortly after the Cromwellian interregnum in England, thereby implying a contemporary moral as regards upending the status quo only to proceed from bad to worse... In *Profile of Clio* and elsewhere Brodsky considers the role of "eschatological dread" and self-interest in human history and how we view it. Brodsky's brilliant but also (in some respects inevitably) unsatisfactory essay on the "Muse of the unique / Historical fact", as Auden called her in *Homage to Clio,* is (like *A King and Not a King)* post-Existentialist – and typically impractical (although *are* there any large-scale practical solutions to the issues Brodsky raises?)... Geoffrey Hill's application of the fable (in *King Log,* 1968) to "the period popularly but inexactly known as the Wars of the Roses" is by implication even more conservative than La Fontaine's, 'King Stork' in his case being little more than Death himself ... The cranes, herons and storks of later versions replace Aesop's water-snake (which reappeared in *Die Wasserschlange* by Lessing, however). The verse-form of *A King and Not a King* is an imitation of Marianne Moore's imitation of La Fontaine's – and a homage to mistress as well as master.

p.119, *"Probably I don't have a style etc."*: Picasso seems to have made this remark in relationship to Jean Cocteau and Erik Satie's surreal ballet, *Parade* (1917), for which he produced the stage-design and costumes, at a time when he was beginning to work simultaneously in a wide variety of styles – or "means of expression" – embracing expressionism, cubism, surrealism, pointillism, post-impressionism, neoclassicism, naturalism, and various sorts and combinations of these, depending on his subject or *motif.* His Cubist colleagues felt abandoned and the critics – not for the first or last time – puzzled. But Picasso's general approach to style was neither to stick with "the same suit of clothes" (which would clearly have bored him) nor to "experiment" according to this or that theory, which he considered "probably the greatest mistake of modern art", but, "when the subject demands a particular means of expression, to use this without hesitation... Whenever I had something to say I said it in the way which seemed right to me. Differing *motifs* demand different methods. This does *not* presuppose evolution or progress, but a correspondence or agreement between the idea one wants to express and the means of expression which is inseparable from it" (*90 Zeichnungen und farbige Arbeiten*, Galerie Beyeler, Basel, 1971, p.24).

p.119, **Two candles dead etc.**: John Richardson (in *A Life of Picasso*, 1991) drew attention to the fact that, if local records are correct, Picasso had a younger brother (named José, after his father) who must have died in infancy. Picasso's beloved younger sister, Conchita, also died – at the age of seven, only a year before the *First Communion* of his surviving sister was painted at his father's instigation. Richardson pointed out that two of the candles on the altar in this picture are lit and two are extinguished: "The candles could … stand for the two living and the two dead children. Combined with the rose-petals, emblems of mortality, that are scattered on the altar steps, this device would suggest that this First Communion is also a *memento mori* that could commemorate the dead Conchita as well as the living Lola." Picasso was born in 1881, Lola (of whom he painted several other remarkable pictures) in 1884.

p.121, **To the upside-down world**: Cp. the song ("To the Looking-Glass world it was Alice that said") in *Through the Looking-Glass*, ch.9… Pointing to Eliot as a precursor of his own (in *Tradition and the Individual Talent*), Borges observed that "Every writer creates his own precursors. His work modifies our conception of the past as it will modify the future." His example of a writer who created more precursors than most is Kafka (in *Kafka and his Precursors*). Of course, the same, or something similar, goes for painters. It comes as a surprise, even so, to find that the Rev. Dodgson can be looked on (in one of the chapters of *Alice* which, coincidentally, influenced Joyce) as a Borgesian 'precursor' of Picasso. In ch.6, His Eg(g)ocentricity, Humpty Dumpty – he who takes the superficially rational but uncommunicative view that "When *I* use a word, it means just what I choose it to mean – neither more nor less" – also advises Alice to try and look a little different:

> "Your face is the same as everybody has – the two eyes, so – " (marking their places in the air with his thumb) "nose in the middle, mouth under. It's always the same. Now if you had the two eyes on the same side of the nose, for instance – or the mouth at the top – that would be some help."
>
> "It wouldn't look nice," Alice objected. But Humpty Dumpty only shut his eyes, and said, "Wait till you've tried."

But Alice has no intention of trying – any more than she has of following his example in the use of words:

> "The question is," said Alice, "whether you *can* make words mean so many different things."

To which Humpty replies at his most Picassian: "The question is … which is to be master – that's all."

p.121, ***Gentleman's wig etc.:*** Referring to various self-portraits and photographs of Picasso, who was notoriously fond of dressing up, especially for guests.

p.122, **Though long before Picasso etc.:** One of Picasso's strengths as a founder of 'modern art' was his awareness of tradition, and *Guernica,* for example, alludes to and adapts subjects and *motifs* from Rubens (above all) and also from antiquity, Raphael, Bartholdi's *Statue of Liberty,* the Christian *Pietá...* In this respect, it was certainly true, as he said himself, that how he painted was basically no different from how any artist had ever painted. What was 'modern' in Picasso – as in other Modernists such as Joyce and Stravinsky – was a clearer (and more articulate) consciousness of other artists' work as an aspect of what he sometimes spoke of as "the outside world", and which Sartre called "facticity", i.e. that which is given. This being the case, Picasso felt at liberty – and had both the ability and vision – to adapt other art more radically or comprehensively (his work was "traditional painting raped", as he provocatively remarked) than most 'traditional' artists would have found acceptable *(90 Zeichnungen,* p.72). He saw his pictures as representations of his, the artist's, idea of 'nature' – a word he used in more than one way, but which, also in the Basel catalogue, he said "is nothing other than a sort of battle between my inner self and the outside world as it exists for most people" – including, by implication, other painters' pictures. Again, this would have interested Sartre, as an exciting example of a 'for-itself' actively constituting a meaningful 'in-itself' of its own. And so, no doubt, would Picasso's no less active apprehension of the fact that – even if 'condemned' to be free – "we *are* a choice and, for us, to be is to choose ourselves" *(Being and Nothingness,* III.2.I). Regretting the absence of a strong and influential school of academic painting in the modern epoch, for example, Picasso said, "There have to be rules, even when they are bad ones, since the strength of art is confirmed in the overcoming of taboos. The removal of all barriers is not freedom but a sort of licentiousness – a boring state of affairs which makes everything spineless, formless, meaningless and trivial." He might have added that the strength of art can also be confirmed in consciously choosing to *conform* to the rules, as he also did, if it should suit one's subject or *motif:* as in life, it is the active nature of the choice which matters – as much as or more than whether one chooses to dissent or not.

p.123, **1656 / 1957**: The subject of this sonnet is the first of Picasso's adaptations of Velasquez' *Las Meninas,* painted in August 1957.

p.124, *1973–1998–????:* Picasso died in 1973.

p.125, **Thirty-Nine Songs (ca. 1250 / 2002):** Most of the poems in this section are loosely based on anonymous poems to be found in: R.T. Davies, *Medieval English Lyrics* (1963), *Totentanz der Stadt Basel (ca.* 1440), Hans Magnus Enzensberger (ed.), *Allerleirauh* (1961) – an outstanding anthology of anonymous German children's rhymes – and James Barke & Sydney Goodsir Smith (ed.s), *The Merry Muses of Caledonia* (1964), which consists for the most part of folksongs collected but not printed by Robert Burns (cp. note on p.132, "My dear, when your husband's away from home"). Two further subsections take as their starting points poems by William

Dunbar, seven are translations from Heine and xxxi is a translation of Goethe's *Erlkönig* (see notes below).

p.125, *"a purely anonymous centre"*: For Rilke, as for Yeats, this included not only "passionate subject-matter" but other areas of human experience which "go beyond the individual", as he put it in another letter, transcending everyday rationality, among other things… Rilke plays an important role in *Then and Now* – especially in *Opus 3*. Here, in his letter to 'R.S.', who had sent him some MSS, emphasizing the fact that he was blind, Rilke acknowledges that any such "great decisive misfortune" must become the centre of the sufferer's "rearranged consciousness". Once this is so, however, one's aim as an artist "should be directed towards enduring this central misfortune more and more without any special name…, preparing it for the freedom of becoming, at certain moments, not misfortune alone but dispensation, privilege." Rilke implies, in other words, that the individual author or artist is free to *achieve* 'anonymity'. An experienced traveller who spent time in several European countries, Rilke felt particularly attuned to the culture of Spain, for example, and it is perhaps no accident that his and Yeats's Spanish contemporary, Miró, also remarked: "Great artistic periods have always been dominated by anonymity. It is becoming more and more necessary today. At the same time, however, one also needs a totally individual gesture. Why? Because a deeply experienced individual gesture *is* anonymous, it opens the door to universality" (Walter Erben, *Miró*, pp.232, 236). In the same interview (in 1959), he said: "In order to become truly human, we must rid ourselves of our false ego. This meant that I had to stop being *Miró*… In other words, one has to aim at anonymity." Miró and Picasso understood each other and each other's art very well, although Miró's view of things is clearly narrower, whereas Picasso's own deeply individual gestures open different doors into many and various areas of the universal: hence, "You see me here but already I've changed and am somewhere else. I'm never tied down."

p.125, *"Talk to me of originality, etc."*: This whole passage is an evident counter-blast to Ezra Pound's catch-phrase *Make it New*. However, Pound (whom Yeats singles out as writing differently from himself) was very capable of using "traditional metres which have developed with the language" (above all, in *Hugh Selwyn Mauberley*), when it suited his project. Moreover, free verse is, obviously, a meaningful and in the meantime venerable form in itself: i.e. the tradition, being by far the greater entity, has subsumed it with no great difficulty – in part, it seems clear, because "traditional metres" are very far from being the *only* form of poetic "salt"… Yeats's view of style may have been more limited than Picasso's (or his subject-matter was): even so, the sheer quality of his poetry effectively quashes, for example, the notion (of which Pound was not entirely innocent) that free verse, like 'modern art', represents some sort of *progress* beyond more traditional verse or art. This notion is still current in some (particularly American or Americanized) circles – sometimes without further consideration, sometimes because "the fashion is the fashion", though "nothing to a man", as two drunken courtiers try to explain to each other in *Much Ado About Nothing*, III.iii. Also still current (if more European) is the – understandable but simplistic – one-hundred-year-old viewpoint *à la* Dada that any means of expression developed within our "botched civilization" (as Pound justifiably called it) is no longer valid because 'tainted' by the worldwide catastrophes which, above all in the twentieth century, have resulted. As a matter of fact, though, this viewpoint (which caused Miró to turn against figurative painting, for instance) implies that one could – and even *should* – not only write or paint but live in some way radically against or outside of or over and above the civilization into which we have been born: tasks beyond practically all of us, even if one were surer than it is possible to be that *minds* would thereby be changed. To change reality we must first of all change how we think about, relate to, act on, and thus help create it. Otherwise – *Plus ça change, plus c'est la même chose*. One might be lucky or unlucky with one's "outside world" – whether political, social or artistic – but the point is *always* to reinterpret its possibilities and re-evaluate what we *do*. The world will then change in so far as it can.

p.125, *"Go, song, etc."*: The *congedo* or 'envoi' of Guido Cavalcanti's *canzone*, *"Donna mi priegha" (ca.* 1290), as translated by Ezra Pound in *Canto XXXVI*. Cavalcanti's famously difficult, and in places obscure, late thirteenth century poem was in effect a challenge to his friend Dante's view of love as embodied (however platonically) in Beatrice… Being greatly susceptible to the power of love, like all sensitive souls, Cavalcanti is acutely aware as well of its inherent dangers and limitations: it is not *virtù*, though of that vein – no matter how beautiful, it is *felt*, not *thought*, and it maintains that affective intention is reason's equal. And so,

> Poor in discernment, being thus vice's friend,
> Often his power meets with death in the end.

Pound's use of translation here as a form of quotation (of which there are, of course, others) is a Modernist device which I have taken over in various ways throughout *Then and Now* (cp. note on p.12, *Heinrich Heine: 'Deutschland. Ein Wintermärchen'*) – in part with the intention of creating an *effect*, at least, of anonymity… Quotation as a means of expression was a major concern of another innovative writer (although not, it seems, a reader of Pound) in the early twentieth century – Walter Benjamin. In the introduction to her important selection of essays by Benjamin, *Illuminations* (1968), Hannah Arendt claims that, from about the mid-1920s, "quotations are at the centre of every work of Benjamin's" – coming, in some cases, to constitute the main work, with his own writing as something secondary… His 1000-page unfinished cultural history of the growth of commodity capitalism in nineteenth century Paris, *The Arcades Project* (on which he worked from 1927 until his death in 1940), consists largely of a vast montage of quotations from hundreds of printed sources, constructed by means of "the craziest mosaic technique you can imagine", as he called it in a letter. As a historical materialist and Marxist – of however peculiar a variety – Benjamin was ultimately aiming, by reconstructing history out of quotations, at an objective image of reality: "the real world," he wrote in *Origin of the German Tragic Drama* (or *'Trauerspiel'*), "could well constitute a task, in the sense that it would be a question of penetrating so deeply into everything real as to reveal thereby an objective interpretation of the world". Benjamin's contemporary, Sartre, however, wrote in *Existentialism is a Humanism* (1946), "we must begin from the subjective". And, whatever the weaknesses of Sartre's essay, his great work *Being and Nothingness* (1943) as a whole takes this proposition as a premiss (cp. note on p.101, *"Man is the only being etc."*). In his long section on what he calls 'The Situation' (IV.1.*II*) Sartre says, "The situation is the subject illuminating things"; it "is a relation of being *between* a for-itself and the in-itself": it 'begins' from the subjective, that is, and ends when the for-itself's 'illumination' of the in-itself ends… If *Then and Now* subscribes in some respects to Benjamin's approach to quotation (and not only in the form of translations), it also remains unrepentantly subjective – a subjective (not autobiographical) variety of epic, even, if "An epic is a poem including history" (Pound, *ABC of Reading*, p.46). Nonetheless, one does not need to agree with Benjamin and Arendt's conviction that an irreparable break in tradition had occurred during the First World War and after to see what Benjamin means by the subversive and even destructive effect which quotations can have across the space between then and now: "Quotations in my work", he wrote, "are like robbers by the roadside who make an armed attack and relieve an idler of his convictions." One ought not to forget, however, that quotations are only one aspect of the vast and complex landscape of intertextuality – as the great Modernists clearly realized – in which we may continue to reap and sow from then to now and from now to then. One might even say that, if anonymity is (or should be) the centre from which art proceeds, the circumference of the sphere which contains and informs it is (or should be) *panonymous* – in so far as the subjective nature of knowledge would permit in the case of each artist.

p.125, **Sing, cuckoo, sing, etc.**: A (winter) version of *Sing! cuccoo nu* was included by Pound – under the title of 'Ancient Music' – in *Lustra* (1916). In *ABC of Reading* (p.14), Pound wrote of his conviction "that music begins to atrophy when it departs too far from the dance; that poetry begins to atrophy when it gets too far from music". A late Romantic in many respects (and, as R.T. Davies remarked, the anonymous lyrics in his anthology have tended to be underrated by "the emphasis put since the romantic movement on originality or spontaneity in poetry and on the personality of the poet"), Pound was nevertheless always sensitive to what he called 'melopoeia' – or the qualities of sound and rhythm in poetry – and celebrated medieval and Renaissance lyricism for this reason. Both he and Eliot were admirers of Dante, for somewhat different reasons. Whereas Pound spoke of "the tremendous music of the *Commedia*", one of Eliot's main interests in the medieval was, of course, religious – and there are many (popular) religious lyrics in Davies's book, which Faber published. The subject-matter of most of its secular lyrics was also the subject-matter, as it happens, of Eliot's *Sweeney Agonistes*:

> SWEENEY: Birth, and copulation, and death.
> That's all, that's all, that's all, that's all,
> Birth, and copulation, and death.
> DORIS: I'd be bored.
> ('Fragment of an Agon', 1947)

The difference, however, is that the medieval lyrics revel – often humorously and/or light-heartedly – in endless variations on these themes, whereas they were (at any rate until *Four Quartets*) too *inherently* anonymous, perhaps, and too corporeal, for Eliot's Romantic / Puritan individualism not to find boring or distasteful on the one hand and (fascinatingly) disgusting on the other.

p.132, **My dear, when your husband's away from home**: The first of six poems in the sequence based on Scottish folksongs from *The Merry Muses of Caledonia* (1800). As well as writing his own poetry, Robert Burns collected several hundred anonymous folksongs during his work as a farmer and while travelling around Scotland as an exciseman. Many of these he rewrote as songs of his own (including some of his most famous) by improving their style, adding or removing stanzas, and in some cases toning down their bawdiness so as to accord with the publishing standards of his day. Some of the songs (presumably also improved by himself) which he found unfit for general circulation were still in a notebook when he died in 1796. This notebook seems to have been lost. However, a version of it, entitled *The Merry Muses of Caledonia,* was published anonymously for an Edinburgh convivial club, the Crochallan Fencibles, of which Burns had been a member. A single copy survives, and has provided a basis for modern editions.

p.133, **My head ached fit to burst last night, etc.**: William Dunbar (ca.1460–1530?) is usually seen as one of the most distinctive of medieval poets. However, he is not only formally a traditionalist but the world-view underlying his verbal fireworks and sense of humour is in most respects that of Everyman. While not generally philosophical, Dunbar is also capable, in poems such as "My heid did yak", "I seik about this world unstabille" (xiv, stanzas 4 & 5) and "Full oft I mus" (xxi), of expressing with moving simplicity the melancholy stoicism of his age – though, for modern tastes, he can be repetitious, hence my excisions.

p.134, **Western wind, etc.**: R.T. Davies dates *Westron winde, when will thou blow?* as "earlier 16c." The historical events behind the original text – possibly part of a longer lyric? – may conceivably be alluded to in Shakespeare's *Henry VIII* (II.i.40–45). In 1520, at any rate, Cardinal Wolsey had the Earl of Surrey dispatched to Ireland as Lord Lieutenant, in order to facilitate a plot to bring down his powerful enemy, the Duke of Buckingham, who was Surrey's father-in-law. Surrey's small army fared badly in the face of local hostility, the plague, and high prices – and morale must have been low ("I and the treasurer with all the captains of the king's retinues here have not between us all 20 pounds in money," Surrey wrote in 1522, after Buckingham's death). It is not difficult to imagine the army, under these circumstances, waiting for a "westron winde" to blow them homeward… The song seems to have been popular – and three masses were composed on the tune, including a famous version by the leading composer of the time, John Taverner, and another (less etherial, perhaps, but no less beautiful) by John Sheppard.

p.138, **On the sands a girl stood sighing, etc.**: A translation of *"Das Fräulein stand am Meere"* – the first of seven translations from Heine, many of whose poems, including this one, were set to music (not always to their benefit) by Romantic composers such as Schubert, Schumann, Mendelssohn, Schoeck. Pound, who published several 'Translations and Adaptations from Heine' in his early book, *Personae* (1909), would no doubt have found that they sang well enough without the music. The other six translations are of *"Still ist die Nacht, es ruhen die Gassen"* (xxix), *Rückschau* (xxxii), *"Ich weiß nicht, was soll es bedeuten"* (xxxvi), *"Nacht lag auf meinen Augen"* (xxxvii), *"In dem Walde sprießt und grünt es"* (xxxviii), *"Mein Tag war heiter"* (xxxix). In each of these (as in most of the translations from Heine in *Opus 1),* I have tried to get as close to the sense and sound of the German as was compatible with writing an English poem. In the case of Heine, one can quote the form of the poetry as well as its sense, since German and English (unlike French or Italian, for example) are relatively 'stress-timed' or isochronous languages and the significance or 'feel' of Heine's metres and stanzas is the same as or very similar to that of their English equivalents… This is one of three sorts of translation in *Then and Now*. The others are, firstly, the *remake* (such as most of the poems in this section, or those based on the anonymous *Totentanz der Stadt Basel* and on German children's rhymes in *Opus 3*) and, secondly, the *adaptation* – for example, of the poems by Heine in *Hamlet in England* (see note on p.103, "But I / Too often see / In my mind's eye"), or of the tales from Boccaccio's *Decameron*, also in *Opus 3*, or from Grimms' *Märchen* throughout the work. In *An East / West Epilogue*, for that matter, there is a straight translation of Lessing's adaptation in *Nathan der Weise* of *Decameron* I, iii (see note on p.180, "Sultan, I am a Jew", §2), framed by a Heinesque adaptation by myself of passages from Edward Gibbon. The difference between the remake and the adaptation is that the former takes a relatively unsophisticated or otherwise defective or only partially appropriate source and simply rewrites or 'borrows' from it, whereas the latter involves the calculated alteration or 'imitation' of an already sophisticated work of art so as to say something about or in addition to it while producing a more or less autonomous text of one's own. More substantial examples of the first than mine would be Shakespeare's use of an entire play by Plautus in *The Comedy of Errors* or of Cinthio's tale of an unnamed Moor of Venice and 'Disdemona' in *Othello;* and of the second, Chaucer's *Knight's Tale* and *Troilus and Criseyde* (both adapted from Boccaccio), Pound's *Homage to Quintus Sextus Propertius*, and (more loosely) Joyce's *Ulysses*. Since they are likely to be some distance in any case from their originals, both remakes and adaptations can validly make use of other people's translations: Shakespeare rewrote Sir Thomas North's *Plutarch* in his Roman plays; Joyce had too little Greek to read Homer's; Eliot adapted the Bible's translation of the Nativity in *Journey of the Magi*. As this implies, both can just as well be of sources in their own language: Shakespeare and *Tristram Shandy* provide examples of the remake, and *Don Quixote* (which universalizes the themes of Spanish romance, among other things) of the adaptation – not to mention my own few stanzas from Gibbon's prose, as noted above, and *Hamlet in England* taken as a whole. Art has always been made of other art, in other words, as well as of life – although to appreciate even an adaptation it may not be *necessary* to know the other art. For example, one does not need to have studied Cervantes' sources to see what he's up to, any more than one needs to have read Boccaccio's *Teseida* to get at least some of the point of Chaucer's *Knight's Tale*.

Of course, a map is not the territory, and most literary categories are no more than a rough guide. Even so, they have their uses. One reason why these particular distinctions, or something like them, are worth drawing with regard to translation is that the failure to do so can easily lead to the slippery slope of rewriting (i.e. treating as raw material for a remake) the kind of highly wrought or thoroughly considered text which demands as close a translation as possible because the more it is changed or interfered with the more it will be spoiled. This "crime of the mind", as Joseph Brodsky called it, tended in his experience to be a question less of incompetence or even indolence than of what he insisted (e.g. with regard to translations of Mandelstam in 'The Child of Civilization', 1977, in *Less Than One*) was the excessive or immature "individuality" of translators: "Their conception of individuality simply precludes the possibility of sacrifice, which is the primary feature of mature individuality (and also the primary requirement of any – even a technical – translation)." Or "...all I want to do is prohibit something I haven't written", as he lamented elsewhere. "How is the reader with no Russian to know," he might have added, "what I wrote and what I didn't write? Or doesn't it matter?" Of the poets quoted in translation in *Then and Now*, Heine and Rilke have suffered notably in this way in recent years... A deliberate adaptation is of course another matter, but on the whole the greater one's source the more important it is that one should have something to *say* by changing it. Otherwise, one is in danger of committing an act of more or less gross disrespect – "at best a sacrilege," to quote Brodsky again, "at worst a mutilation or a murder".

He never said so specifically, as far as I know, but one reason why Brodsky was fighting an uphill battle in the USA in the 1970s and '80s was doubtless the influence of Robert Lowell's controversial book of European poets in English, *Imitations* (1961, 1971), with Ezra Pound's more dubious efforts and opinions in the background *(The Translations of Ezra Pound*, 1970). When it came to translating, Lowell's immature (and, in his case, wilful and self-assertive) individuality may well have been a symptom, at least in part, of the bi-polar or 'manic-depressive' disorder from which he suffered for most of his adult life. In an early, very odd letter (of 2 May, 1936) to Pound, whom he hadn't met, Lowell wrote of his need "to forge my way into reality" – and his difficulties with reality, in a clinical but also everyday sense, are likely to have had an effect as well on how he interpreted the texts in front of him. In a painstaking essay on *Imitations* entitled 'Translation, Imitation, Adaptation, or Mutilation?' Michael Wachtel of Princeton suggests that in many of his letters and in his prose Lowell was "either ... intentionally mystifying his friends and readers or that he wildly overestimated his ability to understand foreign languages." He in fact used cribs of various sorts whenever he could. Even so, it is often difficult, as the essay shows, to distinguish what it euphemistically terms "poetic license" from "fundamental linguistic mistakes" or 'howlers' – which, taken together, constitute a largely unsuccessful attempt, one might say, to forge his way into the reality of other people's poetry... The result, at any rate, was a book consisting for the most part of excessively loose and in places erroneous 'versions', which Heine would have disliked as much as Brodsky. Brodsky's reticence as regards Lowell (although he may have had Lowell's versions of Mandelstam in mind – in *Imitations* and elsewhere – when writing 'The Child of Civilization') was possibly out of gratitude to the senior poet for his help and support when he first arrived as a young exile in the USA in 1972. Also, no doubt, out of respect for (some of) his poetry – which, judging from his fine 'Elegy: For Robert Lowell', he had read closely: more closely, at least, than Lowell had read Heine, for example. Lowell's German was in fact rudimentary and when working on the three 'imitations' which he called *Heine Dying in Paris* he used prose cribs for the first two. In the third, however, he seems to have struggled on his own with the original. The opening lines, for instance, combine what can only be mistranslation with wilful rewriting; the second and third lines, in addition, are in no sense generally true of Heine's poetry or his prose and amount to misinformation; "all sex and thunder" is similarly untrue and as pointlessly vulgar as the second line is pointlessly 'poetic' – the whole remake a cumbersome misrepresentation of the tonal precision, the impeccable style of a perfectly written original.

Heine on Lowell's 'Heine…'

> "My zenith was luckily happier than my night;
> Whenever I touched the lyre of inspiration, I smote
> the Chosen People. Often – all sex and thunder –
> I pierced those overblown and summer clouds…
> But my summer has flowered. Etc. etc."
> – Robert Lowell, 'Heine Dying in Paris' *(Imitations)*

I wasn't "dying", Mr Lowell,
My aim was to live my life and write.
Yours was the irritable bowel,
I saw and said things straight.

I hear you didn't treat your wives
And, worse, your children kindly either.
And your ageing parents? In our lives
Few moral Goods are (mostly) easier.

I begged the Lord – if he wouldn't mind,
Sick as I was – to let me stay
Alive in Paris. How could I find
More beautiful women, anyway,

In the blessed land of Paradise
Than I'd already found on earth:
An angel's wings are very nice,
But nothing to what my wife was worth.

I thanked Him for her happy chatter
And bird-like voice which charmed and amazed
My ears – for how her eyelids fluttered
Around her "good and *faithful*" gaze:

"Perching on cloudlets singing psalms
May be celestial milk and honey,
Dear Lord, but I'm content with the charms
Of earth. Just give me sufficient money –

And please restore my health… I know
The world's a sinful vale of tears.
But I'm used to hard times. Let me go
On shuffling here a few more years.

Far from worldly trouble and strife,
I wear my slippers and dressing-gown
At home together with my wife.
I seldom shuffle, Lord, to town"…

Mein Tag war heiter you mistranslated
Three times. The first and second were worse,
It's true. A poem 'imitated'
From someone else's must converse

With its original, you see,
Not just mis-take it. Willy-nilly,
To falsify reality
Is mad, corrupt, or silly,

And printed text is very real.
One is at liberty to quote –
Adapt – remake it, should one feel
A *need* to. But here's what I wrote:

Cheerful by day and lucky by night,
I've lived and loved. Some praised my songs
And others sang them. Righting wrongs,
They set hearts, bonfires, lust alight.

Summer still blooms, and yet I've brought
My harvest home already. I grieve
For all the loves and lives I must leave
Sooner than ever I'd have thought.

The hand I strummed with sinks – sends flying
A glass which, filled with foaming fizz,
I've often confidently pressed

To laughing lips. How bitter is dying!
O God, how sweet and cosy is
Life in our cosy, sweet little nest!

Two love-birds – but not "stuffed", I hope?
I fear you miss my tone and meaning
In toto. The other two whose scope
You shrank were also more than moaning.

Your sense of irony was not
Subtle enough to read my verse.
When He made your brain the Lord forgot
The humour – anger's playful nurse.

Your "ceaseless alarm-clock" made it hard
(Among much else) to hear the words –
And, worse, the *needs* – of others. Bard
Of dolphins, eels, cod, spiders, birds –

And of the poet's powerful vision –
Which, I'm afraid, contorts, distorts
The world too much too often. Your version
Of what I wrote destroyed my thoughts –

And wrecked my sonnet, needless to say.
Your fourteen liners are merely four-
teen lines: obsessive fragments. My
Rhymes convey meaning, build structures. What's more,

We *always* interpret reality,
But, listen: it's never *all* in the mind.
We have to meet the world halfway:
There's that and this. Who seeks will find

A means to reach the minds of others.
If you win you lose. The American way
Will surely fail. No sisters, no brothers,
You ate your father's balls, shall we say?

And American dreamers yawped – yahooed
Their shocked approval. You told the truth,
They proudly thought. And you thought you'd
Rebelled by shooting off your mouth.

The honest man (I've said elsewhere)
Is the one in – how many? who, more or less,
Knows when he's lying. The *self*-deceiver
Half-hides so as to half-confess.

Such half-truths titillate our wish
To say what we think we think – to do
What we'd really rather not. You fished
For praise and blame – and hooked some, too.

You also misbehaved – and throve
On guilt, like many other 'free'
Achievers in your land. You strove
Bravely to live for poetry.

But Art is analogous to Life –
No more. We're saved by works, not words.
And least of all by blind belief
In God, love, flower-power, the vote, bees/birds…

And yet who dreams the waking dream
Of his life *without* the self-deception
Which blurs the way that how things seem
Shifts with each fear, hope, preconception

Of how they are? We lunge through life
Blindly – fulfil its expectation
Of *more of the past* (less peace, more strife),
Till we stand or fall in resignation:

    (Morphine)

Although one's paler than the other, and
Much sterner – I might almost say much more
Distinguished – than his brother whose arms have held me
Almost intimately – how pleasing and how gentle
His smile was then, how blissful his gaze! – Although
They differ thus, they're also strangely similar,
These two fair youthful figures, one of whom
Has touched my brow with poppies, with the wreath
He wears around his head, whose curious scent
Has driven away the anguish from my soul.
But such relief soon fades. I'll only recover
Completely when the other, gravely, palely
Lowers his torch. Sleep is good. Death is better.
And best would be not to have been born.

Not that things always seemed like that:
My quatrains rhyme, clang, clash or chime,
As did my life… Unfaithful, but
Not deeply – and not all the time –

"God will forgive me. *C'est son métier,*"
Were my last words. But I loved living
So much that Death cannot destroy
The life of my art / the art of my leaving:

All worldly joys have withered away;
My heart has finally had its day,
And my mind has finally had to dispense
With hating evil, even with the sense
Of my own and others' misery –
And death alone's alive in me.

The curtain falls, the performance ends.
My beloved worldly audience wends
Its way back home. They've clapped and laughed
And yawned contentedly. Not daft,
They're off to play or eat and drink
And cuddle before they sleep. I think
Homer's Achilles got it right,
Bewailing his subterranean plight:
"The meanest living philistine
From Passau to Schweinsdorf, from Thames to Tyne,
Is luckier than I, whose blood is shed,
Than I, the Peliad, Prince of the Dead."

Two of Lowell's versions of Heine in *Imitations* are to be found again, slightly improved, in *History*. Both of these books are readily available, together with other texts referred to in the poem, in *Collected Poems* (2003). The three books, *History, For Lizzie and Harriet* and *The Dolphin* (all 1973) in *Collected Poems*, consist of altogether 1246 non-sonnets. (I once knew an artist who was similarly obsessed with A4: everything he did had to be strait-jacketed into that format). In his muddled and self-assertive 'Introduction' to *Imitations*, on the other hand (or 'pole'?), the "strict metrical translators" who, Lowell says, "still exist" but "are taxidermists, not poets, and their poems are likely to be stuffed birds", are the *sort* of translators Brodsky wanted and praised (in 'Ninety Years Later', for example, in *On Grief and Reason*, where J.B. Leishman's rather bland but blank-verse translation of Rilke's *Orpheus. Eurydice. Hermes* is implicitly preferred to Lowell's much looser, not to say slapdash, version, also in *Imitations)*. Lowell writes in his 'Introduction' (which was reprinted, unfortunately, in 1987 in *Collected Prose*) as if there were only two approaches to translating poetry with nothing between them. In practice, he lords it (or, more accurately, tries to lord it) over poets far better than he is – as if to Americanize Europe. The folly – or madness – of this undertaking should be sufficiently apparent... The limitations of Brodsky's view of Leishman's translations of Rilke are considered later, in *Opus 3*. More successfully, he seems to be offering an alternative to Lowell's '91 Revere Street' (written at the suggestion of his psychiatrist) – in particular to its presentation of his Boston Brahmin family and its rejection of his parents, especially (of course) his father – in his modest and moving tribute to his own parents, 'Less Than One' (1976). The poems by Lowell which Brodsky seems to have had admiringly in mind when writing his 'Elegy' include 'The Quaker Graveyard in Nantucket', 'Waking Early Sunday Morning', 'Near the Ocean', 'For the Union Dead'. Nevertheless, his 'Elegy' begins:

> In the autumnal blue
> of your church-hooded New
> England, the porcupine
> sharpens its golden needles
> against Bostonian bricks
> to a point of needless
> blinding shine.

Every word counts here. Likewise in the poem's concluding stanza:

> In the sky with the false
> song of the weathercock
> your bell tolls
> – a ceaseless alarm clock.

p.143, **Who rides so late through the night so wild? Etc.**: *Goethe's Erlkönig* (1782) has been set to music many times – most famously by Schubert in his *Opus 1*. The father/son relationship in the poem anticipates in some respects that of the father and his younger son in section 7, *The Two Sons*.

p.146, **I don't know why things seem / Today so hopelessly sad: / Etc.**: Heine's *Lorelei* poem *("Ich weiss nicht, was soll es bedeuten")* is not based, as one tends to presume, on some ancient Germanic myth but on a poem by his contemporary, Clemens Brentano, who in 1801 published a somewhat longer ballad called *Zu Bacharach am Rheine* in which 'Lore Lay' herself – an enchantress with whom everyone falls in love except the man she wants – plunges to her death in the river. Heine 'borrowed' or, depending on how you see it, stole a number of Brentano's ideas and turned them into one of his best-known lyrics – an act which could only be justified (as in this case) by the sheer quality of what it produced.

p.150, ***From the 2nd edition (1819) of the* Märchen *onwards etc.*:** The earlier editions of the Grimms' collection of folktales (there were seven in all, the last in 1857) were not primarily intended for children. In later editions, many tales were more or less rewritten with children in mind, but not all... *Der Räuberbräutigam*, for example, became less rather than more suited to the nursery when further material was added to Marie Hassenflug's.

p.150, **In Hanau, on the Kinzig, there once lived / A miller**: The Kinzig is an 80-mile tributary of the Maine, into which it flows somewhat to the west of Hanau. The biggest mill on the river was for centuries the Herrenmühle, in the oldest part of Hanau, where the miller of *The Bride's Story* presumably lived. Before reaching Hanau, the Kinzig flows through the extensive natural forest known as the Bulau. A few miles up the river from the mill is one of its few (wooden) footbridges, the Kinzigsteg – which comes into the poem. The bridge was formerly used by swineherds, the citizens of Hanau having long been permitted to fatten their pigs in the forest...

p.151, **His family had been Huguenots**: Calvinist refugees from France and the Spanish Netherlands had made a significant contribution to Central and North German prosperity since the sixteenth and seventeenth centuries. Like other Puritans in other places, they tended to interpret material prosperity as a sign that the Lord was with them – and eventually, in many cases, to value prosperity as much as or more than the Lord.

p.151, **Maria was her name: / She also pondered**: Cp. "But Mary kept all these things, and pondered them in her heart" *(Luke II.19)*. What's in a name? More perhaps in some than in others. Was a Catholic girl ever named Mary without consequence? Even Captain Fox may have found the name of interest.

p.154, *A new commandment I give unto you..., etc.:* Jesus's radical reinterpretation of the Jewish Law and inversion of pagan values – in particular Roman materialism and ruthlessness – might in fact have turned the (Western) world upside down, were it not for the human capacity to say or even *believe* one thing and do another. For certain societies and individuals at certain times, of course, Jesus's teaching has always seemed to offer the world a future. In the East, the Buddha's had already done so – five hundred years earlier (see *Opus 3, No.3*, section 14, ii, 'Siddhartha and Others')... The Biblical quotations (slightly adapted in some cases) are from *John XIII.34, John XV.13, Mark XIV.23–24, Mark VIII.35*, respectively. The priest might have added, in this context, "Blessed are the merciful" *(Matthew V.7)* – and, in all seriousness, the preceding verse: "Blessed are they who hunger and thirst after righteousness, for they shall be filled."

p.155, **as if, in Holy Week, to defile / Easter itself**: If Maria was right and Fox was really so insane as to see himself as a sort of Anti-Christ, he may well have been aware that – as is still the case in parts of Central Germany (for example, around Heidelberg) – the Wednesday on which he (less casually than appears?) arranged to meet Maria at the Kinzigsteg was known as *Krummer Mittwoch* (Crooked Wednesday) because it was the day on which Judas arranged to betray Jesus, as he – Fox – intended to betray Maria's trust. Far-fetched though this may seem, "The devil can cite Scripture for his purpose", as Jesus himself (cp. *Matthew IV.6*) as well as Shakespeare knew. Moreover, the following day, *Gründonnerstag* (Maundy Thursday), was the day of the Last Supper, the Eucharist and the "new commandment" ("...that ye love one another, as I have loved you") – whereas Fox intended, with Maria in his possession, only "to steal and to kill and to destroy".

p.161, ***The Two Sons:*** Jesus' famous 'parable' is virtually a fable, though more enlightened (as one would expect) than those deriving from Aesop (cp. next note but one). There is an important group of *Märchen* also which involves young men or women leaving home to seek their fortune... The parable's usual and somewhat misleading title in English ('The Prodigal Son') seems to have originated from a marginal note in a sixteenth century edition of the Vulgate. Its meanings are many, but regardless of how one interprets it, all three main characters matter. Jesus left his listeners to imagine for themselves *what happened next*.

An East / West Epilogue

p.167, ***Words are not just wind:*** Cp. note on p.193, *After Chuang Tzu*.

p.169, ***"Give not that which is holy unto the dogs, etc.":*** An unusually exclusive saying on the part of Jesus – although, dogs and pigs being unclean but relatively intelligent animals, one which needs little explanation (in *Fables* II, 18 – in which a cat becomes a woman but continues to hunt mice – La Fontaine writes "You've tried to reform what will not learn"). Other Biblical references in *Aesopean (3)* are to be found in vi and ix: cp. notes below. The fables associated with Aesop himself are, as already noted, remarkable for their knowing cleverness and understanding of human weakness and folly – but not for what one might think of as Christian or enlightened Eastern values, nor even for pagan heroism or magnanimity. The closest they get to altruism is 'one good turn deserves another', and the idea of forgiveness is entirely foreign to them. Hence, at least in part, Borges' dismay when he realized in 1941 that "we are *in* the rudimentary world of the slave Aesop"... And now?

p.169, **As if two travellers crossed a land / Inhabited only by monkeys**: This fable probably dates back to Phaedrus, via a medieval French collection of fables. Elsewhere Phaedrus introduces a fox who (unlike the first traveller) makes it clear what she thinks of monkeys:

> A monkey asked a fox for some of her tail,
> To cover his indecently naked buttocks...

p.171, **But honey / Was shortly found in his carcass**: In *Judges XIV.5–9*, the young Samson is attacked by a lion, which he kills. Later he finds that "there was a swarm of bees and honey in the carcase of the lion" – and eats of the honey. But Samson misuses his God-given strength: "It is not good to eat much honey: so for men to seek their own glory is not glory" *(Proverbs XXV.27)*. However, the Bible is ambivalent as regards honey, and in several places it is compared to wisdom or understanding: "My son, eat thou honey..., which is sweet to thy taste:

So shall the knowledge of wisdom be to thy soul: when thou hast found it, then there shall be a reward" *(Proverbs XXIV.13–14)*.

p.173, **By bread alone / We die**: According to the Gospels, what Jesus said was: "It is written, Man shall not live by bread alone, but by every word which proceedeth out of the mouth of God" *(Matthew IV.4)*.

p.175, ***Nathan the Wise:*** The middle segment of this section is a translation of Act III, sc. 4–7 of G.E. Lessing's *Nathan der Weise* (1779). Of this popular classic Heine – who had the greatest respect for Lessing – wrote in *On the History of Religion and Philosophy in Germany* (1835) that it was not only a good comedy but also a philosophical and theological discourse in favour of deism (the belief in a divine Creator who then refrained from intervening in the world). Be this as it may, I have used the verse-form of *Deutschland. Ein Wintermärchen* for the opening and closing sections of the 'medley'… In the 'Paralipomena' to *Nathan*, Lessing admitted to disregarding historical accuracy to suit his own purposes. However, he seems to have envisaged the action of his play (whose scene is Jerusalem) as taking place, roughly speaking, during some pause in the siege of St. John of Acre (or Ptolomais) in 1189–91. A number of the details – and also the quotations at the end – are taken from Gibbon's *Decline and Fall of the Roman Empire*, ch. LIX . Borges regarded Gibbon as a classical writer with as good as no interest in or premonition of "the romantic discovery of the personality" in which "all of us are now so absorbed that the fact of denying or neglecting it is only one of many clever ways of 'being personal'." Even so, the eloquent and humane conclusion of ch. LIX of his history, for example, is imbued with "an incredulity which is not devoid", as Borges observed as well, "of indulgence and, perhaps, compassion."

p.175, **"*Man baute nicht Rom an einem Tag*"**: "Rome wasn't built in a day", Barbarossa's words in *Deutschland. Ein Wintermärchen* (l.1075) – appropriate in that his aim as Emperor was to re-establish German power in Italy. The line is characteristic, too, of the well-documented German tendency (cp. Lessing's story of the rings, which follows) to take a very long-term view of things… Heine first of all presents Barbarossa as the hero of a Romantic *Märchen*, and then (typically) mocks his militarism, while implying the potential consequences for modern Germany…

p.177, **To calm him, Sittah says, "Perhaps / They simply couldn't find him"**: These two lines, which could be the first half of another quatrain, form a metrical bridge into the translation of Lessing's play. A competent but not particularly gifted writer of verse, Lessing (unlike Heine or Rilke, for example) is not always able to load every rift with ore. A line-for-line translation of his 'blank verse' into English blank verse results almost unavoidably in adding, padding and thinness of texture, to avoid which and retain as much of the work's poetry as possible, I have shortened Lessing's metre for the most part to a three- or four-beat line.

p.180, **Sultan, / I am a Jew**: Many eighteenth century German cities imposed severe restrictions on the residence and activities of Jews. Lessing valued tolerance – and opposed all forms of anti-semitism. But the role of Christianity in the Age of Enlightenment also preoccupied him. His obvious integrity as well as his intellect and creative abilities saw to it that by the end of the following century his reputation as a German classic was established, although still controversial. In 1922 *Nathan der Weise* was filmed in what later became Munich's Bavaria Film Studios. After an unsuccessful attempt to ban it, the NSDAP tried in October to get hold of the reels and destroy them – again unsuccessfully. The film was then shown in January 1923 to enthusiastic audiences in Berlin. In Munich the only cinema which dared to include it in its programme, *Regina Lichtspiel,* received a phonecall during the premiere informing its owner that if he tried to show it again the following evening "his flea-pit would be smashed to pieces". The SA was already active in Munich (the so-called Beer Hall *Putsch* took place in November of that year) and after the film had been attacked in the *Völkischer Beobachter,* the cinema withdrew it.

Lessing's plot adapts Boccaccio's *Decameron* I, iii – a vaguely anti-semitic tale in which Melchizedek the Jew, a rich money-lender from Alexandria, evades the quarrel which Saladin attempts to pick with him as an excuse for confiscating his possessions. Saladin, who has resolved "to use force disguised as fiction", asks Melchizedek which of the three laws he considers the true one. When he perceives that "the fellow had cleverly got round the trap he had set him" by using the story of the rings to claim that "the question of which of God's peoples possesses the true faith remains in abeyance and has never been settled", Saladin is impressed, treats Melchizedek with respect and they become friends. There is no suggestion that the tale reveals a higher truth. In fact the preceding tale tells (albeit humorously) "how [the Jew] Abraham's soul was saved" by his becoming a Christian. In the medieval mind, at any rate, there was no doubt as to "Which of the faiths, which of the laws, / … brought … most enlightenment."

As for Heine, he was mainly interested in *Religion and Philosophy in Germany* in what he saw as Lessing's step away from (medieval and then Lutheran) religion towards the philosophy of Kant and above all Hegel, whom he had heard lecture in Berlin on history and dialectics – that is, on how history proceeds through conflict and reconciliation out of which grow further conflict and further reconciliation, and so on in successive stages towards the consciousness of freedom. Through all these phases of what we may now prefer to think of as forms of gradual cultural *change,* not necessarily improvement, Heine discerned the working of a principle which is surely true of *any* culture – namely, that our thoughts resemble a soul (as he put it) which demands a body: "Thought seeks to become action, the word to become flesh… The world is the signature of the word."

p.188, **One hundred thousand Christians died**: This is Gibbon's figure, in *Decline and Fall* ch. LIX, and is probably as (in)accurate as any other (estimates of how many people died in the Crusades – "this holy madness", as Gibbon calls them – vary between 1 and 9 million).

p.190, **The infidel horde was even convinced / *Coeur de Lion* was a cannibal**: The story of Richard I's cannibalism is told in the fourteenth century romance, *Richard Coer de Lyon* – which was probably based on an earlier Norman original. Anyone with a copy of Scott's *The Talisman* will find the relevant sections of this poem translated in the introductory notes, where it reads like a piece of medieval English propaganda for scaring Saracens.

p.193, **After Chuang Tzu:** Most of the poems in this section have been adapted from the writings of Chuang Tzu. According to his translator Burton Watson, Chuang Tzu (Master Chuang) lived from about 369 to 286 BC. A philosopher with the style and stylishness of a poet, he may have been the first Chinese writer to formulate and elaborate on the Taoist way of thinking. He seems to have been born in the state of Sung, which was never an important state and "led a precarious existence, constantly invaded or threatened by more powerful neighbours", with its weakness much aggravated by internal strife. The political and social oppression and insecurity which resulted may help to account for the scepticism and mystical detachment of Chuang Tzu, his concentration on the inner freedom of the individual from "a world dominated by chaos, suffering and absurdity" (Watson)… For Westerners (and no doubt many modern Chinese), Chuang Tzu's writing is not easy. One reason for this is the precise (or imprecise) meaning of certain key terms, such as the Way, Nature, Mind, Knowledge, Truth, Virtue, Clarity. Moreover, one of his favourite games is to question the use and/or validity of words – in general and in particular… This and his fondness for irony can make it difficult to know quite how to take him. Another reason for Chuang Tzu's difficulty is that, unlike the Buddha (see *Opus 3, No.3*, section 14, ii), he has no interest in explaining *how* one is to achieve the enlightened states of mind of which he speaks (he was addressing a "spiritual élite", Watson says, whose main aim was to refine their already high level of understanding). He states his conclusions, rather than how he arrived at them, which can leave one feeling distinctly lost or out of one's depth. In some respects, the stories or parables which are scattered throughout his writings – and which resemble Aesop's fables in their humour, if not in how they see things – are the most approachable sections of them, and it is on these that the sequence concentrates. Without Aesop as a model, the sequence would not have taken the form it does: hence *Aesopean (4)*.

p.197, **Chuang Tzu dreamed / He *was* the butterfly**: The nature of reality is a recurring theme in the writings of Borges, and it would have been surprising if a mind of the type and calibre of Chuang Tzu's had gone unnoticed in them. The narrator of Borges' story, *The Garden of Forking Paths* (1941) is himself Chinese and an illustrious ancestor is the author of the story within the story, a seemingly chaotic novel (cp. note on p.109, "the forking paths"), rescued from oblivion on the death of its author by a Taoist monk. The key to the novel's structure, as noted, is the nature of time. Three or four years later, Borges discussed Chuang Tzu's butterfly dream in *A New Refutation of Time* (1944–1947). In this long essay he proposes that if space does not exist (as Berkeley and other idealist philosophers have argued), then time does not exist either. *"And yet, and yet…"* he concludes (inserting these four words, in his otherwise Spanish text, in English): "Denying temporal succession, denying the self, denying the astronomical universe, are apparent desperations and secret consolations… Time is the substance of which I am made. Time is a river which sweeps me along, but I am the river; it is a tiger which destroys me, but I am the tiger; it is a fire which consumes me, but I am the fire. The world, unfortunately, is real; I, unfortunately, am Borges." Chuang Tzu's response to this would no doubt have been that it depends on how you take it (cp. also *Opus 3, No.1,* section 11, v, 'The Blessing'). When it comes to butterflies and toads, however, who would *not* endorse Borges' "unfortunately"?